AGO-IWOYE
Chronicles of Heritage and Resilience

HRM ABDULRAZAQ ADESHINA ADENUGBA
EBUMAWE OF AGO-IWOYE

AGO-IWOYE

Chronicles of Heritage and Resilience

OLATUNJI OLUSANYA

AGO-IWOYE: CHRONICLES OF HERITAGE AND RESILIENCE
By Olatunji Olusanya

Copyright © 2025 by Olatunji Olusanya

Published by Baruch Publishing - 07908684207
Contact Copyright Holder at
Olatunji Olusanya
Email: tunjat045@yahoo.com
Tel: 07403 232433

All rights are reserved. No part of this publication may be reproduced, stored in a retrieval system or transmitted in any form or by any means, electronic, mechanical, photocopying, recording or otherwise, without prior permission of Olatunji Olusanya

Cover & Interior Design by Karl Hunt

ISBN 979-8-89686-413-4

CONTENTS

Dedication vii
Preface ix
Introduction xi

CHAPTER 1: My Childhood — 1

CHAPTER 2: Weekend Trips in Ago-Iwoye — 12

CHAPTER 3: The Composition of the Town — 17

CHAPTER 4: Politics in Ago-Iwoye — 25

CHAPTER 5: The Kingship of Ago-Iwoye — 31

CHAPTER 6: Forced Marriage in Ago-Iwoye — 41

CHAPTER 7: Child Head Injection Rumour — 47

CHAPTER 8: Children's Fun Moments — 51

CHAPTER 9: Youths' Night Hangout — 54

CHAPTER 10: Government's Well (Idi Konga) Ishamuro — 58

CHAPTER 11: The Social Party People — 62

CHAPTER 12: The Village Life 66

CHAPTER 13: The Eight Quarters of Ago-Iwoye 70

CHAPTER 14: Village Vibes After Dusk 74

CHAPTER 15: Religious Activities in Ago-Iwoye 77

CHAPTER 16: Mother's Roles 81

CHAPTER 17: The Annual Traditional Festival 85

CHAPTER 18: Modern Christianity 93

CHAPTER 19: Speaking Volumes Through the Eyes 97

CHAPTER 20: Uncommon Experiences in Ago-Iwoye 100

CHAPTER 21: Tales of My Hometown 106

CHAPTER 22: Living in a Glass House 109

CHAPTER 23: The Life of Ajamiroku 114

CHAPTER 24: Mushafau: The Disabled Bicycle Repairer and Rental 117

CHAPTER 25: Iwoye Town Centre 123

CHAPTER 26: The Causes of Teenage Ritualism 128

CHAPTER 27: Ago-Iwoye: A Legacy of Agriculture, Trade, and Cultural Heritage 135

CHAPTER 28: The History of Naming Age Groups (Egberegbe) 139

Other Books by the Author 144
About the Author 145

DEDICATION

To the resilient people of Ago-Iwoye, past and present, whose courage, unity, and stories have shaped the essence of this remarkable town.

To the memory of our forebears, who laid the foundation of our heritage with wisdom and sacrifice. And to the generations yet to come, may this work inspire you to honour and preserve the rich legacy of our shared history.

PREFACE

The inspiration for this work arises from a personal journey of rediscovery. Having been born and raised in Ago-Iwoye, I witnessed firsthand the vibrant communal life and the transformative moments that shaped the town. These experiences left an indelible impression on me and a profound appreciation for the intricacies of our heritage.

Writing this book has been an act of preserving memories and passing down history to future generations. It is both a tribute to the people of Ago-Iwoye and a gift to those who seek to understand the foundational narratives that have defined our identity.

In these pages, you will encounter stories of hardship and hope, of ordinary lives touched by extraordinary circumstances. You will see how our forebears navigated political transitions, embraced religious harmony, and developed an unwavering commitment to collective progress. These accounts remind us of the importance of community, tradition, and adaptability in the face of changing times.

As we venture through these recollections, I invite you to immerse yourself in the stories that shaped Ago-Iwoye and appreciate the enduring lessons they impart. This book is for the past, present, and future, anchoring our shared identity in the rich soil of memory and culture.

INTRODUCTION

Ago-Iwoye stands as a bastion of history and heritage in Ijebuland, representing a town shaped by a legacy of tradition, resilience, and cultural pride. This book is an attempt to capture the essence of a community whose evolution has been marked by both the turbulence of change and the enduring influence of its past. Drawing on vivid recollections of a bygone era, it provides a rich tapestry of anecdotes, historical contexts, and societal reflections that form the heart of Ago-Iwoye's narrative.

By delving into various dimensions of the town's development–its unique customs, political landmarks, religious inclusivity, and the vibrant lives of its residents–this book serves as both a memoir and a historical document. From the dynamics of its quarters to the tales of notable figures and communal rituals, each page brings to life the intricate connections that bind the town's people, past and present.

More than just a chronicle of events, this book illuminates the threads of culture, education, and family values that have sustained Ago-Iwoye through the decades, offering readers a lens into the triumphs and trials of its history.

CHAPTER ONE
MY CHILDHOOD

Ago-Iwoye was once recognised as the fourth-largest town in Ijebuland. At that time, Ijebuland, as geographically defined, included Ikorodu and Epe, which were part of Ijebu before being incorporated into Lagos State during its creation. This merger was intended to expand Lagos in terms of landmass and population. Historically, Ijebuland shared boundary lines with Ibadan, the capital of Oyo State, and with the Egba people. The largest town in Ijebuland was Ijebu-Ode, followed by Shagamu in Remoland.

There have been ongoing agitations among local interest groups advocating for the independent status of Remoland, separate from Ijebuland. This tension often manifested in disputes over royal supremacy between the Awujale of Ijebu-Ode and the Akarigbo of Shagamu in Remoland. To maintain political stability, a resolution was reached to divide the two provinces, ensuring neither claimed superiority over the other.

One notable factor I observed during my childhood in Ago-Iwoye in the 1940s and 1950s was the absence of public transportation within the town. While there were a few transport garages, these served exclusively as hubs for travellers journeying beyond the town's borders. These garages acted as gathering points for passengers embarking on outward journeys or as designated locations where vehicles dropped off passengers at the end of their trips.

When I was growing up, a significant transport garage was located at Okebute Junction, where Idode Road intersected with the road from Okelusote near Pepelu House. This garage was neither a purpose-built facility nor equipped with any infrastructure; rather was an open space situated at the intersection of major roads. It was not an official designation by any council or township authority but emerged as a convenient location for residents from various parts of the town to converge and board transport.

The vehicles departing from this garage typically travel through Oru en route to destinations such as Ijebu-Igbo, Ijebu-Ode, and onwards to Lagos or Ibadan via Mamu. Oru, being a prominent junction, offered trading opportunities for the local populace, who engaged in petty trading activities.

Ago-Iwoye also featured several roads connecting it to surrounding villages and notable landmarks. These included the Okebute roads, the Okodo roads linking to the Ome River (which runs behind the Olabisi Onabanjo University campus), the Imere Road leading to Ago-Iwoye Secondary School, and the Ishamuro Road, which provided access to the Christian and Muslim burial grounds.

Ago-Iwoye is home to numerous villages, too many to mention here at the moment. However, I will try to highlight some of them later in this, especially where history links them to significant social and trading activities of the town. Travelling to these villages at the time was done on foot, carrying agricultural produce to the market on one's head. For fear of being attacked, either by dangerous elements–who were common and rampant then–travellers heading in the same direction often gathered at a designated spot and commenced their journeys together.

It was interesting to journey with others, especially when they were related, shared something in common, came from the same or neighbouring villages, or were headed to the same destination or market to sell goods. These trips were made lively by the stories narrated by travellers, which ranged from personal experiences to tales they had heard or imagined. It was surprising how quickly time passed when surrounded by like-minded individuals.

At that time, the township had no internal transport system operating solely within its borders. Taxi services were non-existent, and people moved from place to place on foot without feeling pain, fatigue, or boredom, nor did they fear attacks from unknown persons, as is common today. Virtually everyone knew each other–either by name, through family connections, age groups known as *Egberegbe*, social activities, or neighbourhood interactions.

The upbringing instilled in us by our parents emphasised respect for all older individuals, regardless of the age gap. Moreover, it was a societal expectation to greet others with the utmost cheerfulness. Anyone who felt you had failed in this duty could reprimand you or even report you to your parents. Such a report often resulted in being disciplined, as a failure to exhibit good manners or proper home training was considered unacceptable.

Fatherhood was not limited to one's biological father. All our uncles were referred to as fathers, and all members of our fathers' age groups were collectively called 'fathers.' It was only when identifying them in relation to their children that you would specify, such as 'father of so-and-so.'

The township of Ago-Iwoye was highly regarded for its community of business magnates, whose principal ventures revolved around ownership of public transport. These vehicles bore distinctive names boldly inscribed on their sides. Most public transport vehicles at the time featured wooden cabins for passengers, commonly referred to as *Bole Kaja*, which literally translates to 'get down and fight.' Owners who did not drive their vehicles personally took great care in selecting drivers, valuing reputation above all. Suitable drivers, eager for employment, would often boast of their experience, detailing the number of accidents they had encountered and proudly attributing their survival to either driving skill or the protective powers of traditional native charm.

Transport vehicles of that era could be graded or categorised in various ways, and I can recall the names of some prominent transport operators in Ago-Iwoye during the period in question. The foremost operators were the twin brothers from Odosinusi, renowned as reputable cocoa produce buyers and commercial transport owners. Their surname was Quadri, and they were widely recognised throughout the town. They branded their vehicle with the name *ORE MEJI*–meaning 'two friends'–and hired drivers with a shared commitment to safeguarding their esteemed reputation. Their wooden vehicles, typical of the *Bole Kaja* design, promised a level of comfort akin to that of British Airways today, albeit without food and drink service. Notably, their vehicles were never associated with serious accidents, suggesting a meticulous selection process for their drivers.

Another prominent transporter of note was a man popularly known as Bude. While his actual name remains unknown, his professionalism, dedication, and prominence in the 1950s made him a significant figure in Ago-Iwoye. Bude owned and drove his vehicle, employing conductors who served as apprentices learning the trade. His conductors provided exceptional customer service, often going to great lengths to assist regular passengers with their belongings, such as carrying baskets from customers' homes to the parked vehicle. In return, appreciative customers, including my sister, would often tip the conductors out of goodwill, beyond the standard fare. This act of generosity fostered healthy competition among conductors for the privilege of assisting valued customers.

The most flamboyant transport operators of the time were another pair of brothers, the Ogunekos. The elder brother, Baba Ade, was particularly charismatic. He used a signature trumpet to announce his arrival and departure, with a self-composed chant that went: 'Iya Ade teba demi ko yi gari o', meaning 'Ade's Mum, prepare starchy cassava food for me, and make it soft.' His vehicles bore the simple yet distinctive name *Baba Ade*. Baba Ade was gentle, with an impeccable driving record and a courteous demeanour towards customers. He maintained regular routes between market towns such as Ijebu-Ode and Mamu, driven by his dedication to providing for his immediate family.

His younger brother, nicknamed *ALL PEACE,* operated under a similarly commendable ethos. Together, these brothers exemplified the high standards of professionalism and customer care that were hallmarks of Ago-Iwoye's transport operators during this era.

The most notable and consistently talked-about figure was his brother, Paul, as previously mentioned. Known universally by his nickname, *All Peace*, he was extremely popular. This moniker was inscribed on the side of his vehicle, marking his identity across the regions he traversed. Paul's reputation extended beyond mere recognition; he was the subject of much discussion for various reasons.

Unlike other transport operators who worked within Yorubaland, Paul's route took him to the northern parts of the country, transporting bundles of kola nuts packed in baskets along with their traders to places such as Sokoto, Kano, and Funtua, among others. He not only owned the vehicle but also drove it himself. However, the nickname *All Peace* stood in stark contrast to his lifestyle.

To different people, Paul was a man of many faces. His arrogant demeanour often matched his impressive physical stature and first-class personality. Within his age group, he was held in high regard and often considered a wealthy man. While many allegations were levelled against him, no one dared to confront him directly, owing to the intimidating esteem in which he held himself. His family house was almost directly opposite ours, across the road. This proximity offered us an intimate knowledge of the people in their household, a relationship borne of what we termed *neighbourhood intimacy*. Paul had a younger brother who was of the same age as me. We often played ball together and engaged in occasional mischief, reflecting the juvenile delinquencies of youth. I was a regular visitor to their family house, and he was just as familiar with ours.

This narrative would not be complete or true to my desire for authenticity without mentioning their father, Pa Oguneko. He was a well-known and feared figure in the Idode quarters, serving for many years as the night guard of the Okebute area. Under his watch, there was not a single report of goats being stolen or houses being robbed, regardless of how secluded the location was.

Pa Oguneko's nightly whistle-blowing began at 11pm., a warning for residents to return indoors. By midnight, anyone found wandering risked dire consequences. While the penalties rarely involved death, offenders could be left incapacitated through various deformities, mental illnesses, or physical disabilities. His reputed use of black magic created an air of fear. Tales abounded of his ability to inflict permanent conditions on those who flouted the curfew.

Given his nocturnal profession, he was seldom seen during the day, a mystique that fuelled rumours about his life. Even casual conversations with him were avoided by the community, and his children were similarly regarded with trepidation. Their peers, and even their teachers, treated them cautiously, fearing possible repercussions from their father's supernatural capabilities. This defied the usual principle that all students were equal before the school rules and regulations.

The Ago-Iwoye community was rife with unsubstantiated yet humorous rumours. Stories were told of night guards transforming into cats or disappearing to evade attackers, only to reappear and launch counterattacks from unexpected positions. Another tale claimed that Pa Oguneko could shoot his locally made Dane gun while it pointed at himself and still hit his intended target unerringly. It was also said that a liquid he used to wash his face enabled him to foresee and intercept robberies before they occurred. Such accounts, whether true or exaggerated, contributed to a significant reduction in crime in the area.

The town of Ago-Iwoye has since undergone remarkable transformations, both in infrastructure and societal outlook. Civilisation and modern development have brought change to its inhabitants. The Ebumawe's palace, once a modest structure, has been relocated to a spacious area in Okelusote. A new palace, reflecting the community's pride and status, has been erected, becoming a hub for dignitaries and ceremonial homage.

Interestingly, the new palace occupies land that was once home to the town's dispensary and maternity hospital, spanning from Idode Road at Okebute to Okelusote Road. However, in typical Nigerian fashion, some portions of the palace's reserved land have been appropriated for private developments. The imposing gates and inscriptions on the new palace confer upon the town a renewed sense of prestige.

Secondly, profound thanks are due to the late Olabisi Onabanjo, a one-time civilian governor of Ogun State. During his tenure, he employed liberal political discretion to establish Ogun State University, designating Ago-Iwoye as its administrative headquarters and campus. This development catalysed infrastructural growth in various parts of the town. Students from diverse backgrounds arrived to receive an education, bringing their cultures and traditions to complement those inherited from past generations. Consequently, small businesses thrived, trades flourished, and many locals experienced economic upliftment through petty trading.

However, the influx of students also introduced certain challenges. Problems such as cultism, internet fraud (Yahoo Yahoo), and other social vices tarnished the community's image, spreading fear among lecturers, students, and residents. The peace and tranquillity Ago-Iwoye once enjoyed were disrupted. A particularly grim episode saw the palace attacked, with lives tragically lost during the unrest–an unfortunate chapter in the town's history. Frequent incidents of gun violence among the student population resulted in innocent bystanders losing their lives while going about their daily activities.

Political transitions inevitably bring about policy changes. Otunba Daniel, another former governor of Ogun State, relocated several departments of the state university to other towns. This was ostensibly done to promote fairness, reduce overcrowding, and address spatial constraints. The initial plan relocated Medicine and Medical Sciences to Sagamu and Agriculture to Ayetoro. However, in a bid to consolidate his political influence, Governor Daniel allocated other departments to various towns, often disregarding the economic viability or conduciveness of these locations.

When most departments were situated in Ago-Iwoye, both indigenes and non-indigenes saw opportunities for economic growth. Locals expanded their homes, constructing new structures to accommodate incoming students. Meanwhile, non-indigenous residents and workers in the town secured bank loans to build modern housing for students, lecturers, and other staff of the university. Unfortunately, the relocation of departments under Daniel's administration dashed these aspirations. Many construction projects were abandoned, loans went unpaid, and escalating interest rates compounded the financial distress. Thriving petty traders faced diminished demand, leading to the collapse of their businesses.

While this book does not aim to delve into politics, addressing occurrences and omissions often invites criticism from beneficiaries of past regimes. Accusations, verbal abuse, and even threats can be expected as part of democratic and political discourse. As the saying goes, *truth is bitter*, and wisdom teaches that a lack of tension in private familial discussions often signals untruths.

At one point, the Ogun State government attempted to increase the number of local councils under its jurisdiction. One proposed council was Ifelodun Local Council, with Ago-Iwoye slated as its headquarters, and surrounding towns such as Oru, Awa, and Mamu included within its jurisdiction. This council was to be carved out of the existing Ijebu North East Local Council, which is headquartered in Ijebu-Igbo. However, the proposal was rejected by the federal government, citing insufficient grassroots support–an outcome influenced by the disunity and lack of consensus among political heavyweights, including the Awujale of Ijebu-Ode.

The Awujale's stance is somewhat understandable; the people of Ijebu-Ode have long sought to annex Mamu into their local council. This claim is tenuous, as Mamu, founded by the last *Bale* Ato of Idode, has no cultural, traditional, or historical links to Ijebu-Ode. The geographical distance between the two towns is significant, separated by numerous villages with distinct identities. Nevertheless, the Awujale's influence carries substantial weight in Ogun State's decisions concerning Ijebuland.

The aspirations for the creation of the Ifelodun Local Council remain compelling, given the area's population, size, and economic potential. The local council could likely sustain itself with its resources, provided there is sufficient political will from the state government to push the proposal forward. The efforts of Honourable Segun Adesegun, former deputy governor and commissioner, have demonstrated a commitment to the area's independence. It is hoped that these aspirations will not fade into oblivion.

Ultimately, justice must be seen to be done, guided by fairness and equity.

CHAPTER TWO

WEEKEND TRIPS IN AGO-IWOYE

Earlier in 2024, driven by curiosity, I seized an opportunity during a visit to my birthplace to spend a day exploring my family village, which I had not seen in over seventy years. The state where I found the town was shocking and profoundly disheartening–a shadow of its former self, marked by emptiness and neglect. It starkly contrasted to the vibrant and flourishing community I remembered from the 1940s and '50s.

The village, an ancestral heritage of my family, forms part of a division into two quarters. Each quarter had numerous buildings, albeit not constructed with bricks or blocks as is commonplace today. Instead, the houses were traditionally built using mud. These villages served as year-round residences for families engaged in farming activities, forming a vital part of their livelihood. The township of Ago-Iwoye itself encompassed more than two hundred villages established by different families. Each adult male head of a family could own between five and ten farmland plots, cultivating crops deemed most promising for financial stability. These plots were typically inherited from fathers or, in some cases, great-grandfathers, depending on the historical circumstances of the family.

Traditionally, most adult males maintained a hut in the village for their immediate family, offering privacy and independence. The size and structure of these huts depended more on financial capability than the size of the household. Notably, many grandfathers and fathers in our community had a minimum of four wives. This practice, while aligned with religious doctrine, also symbolised social prestige and responded to maternal pressures to enhance familial status.

Islam was the predominant religion among my family members, with approximately ninety-nine per cent adhering to the faith. However, levels of commitment varied. While some embraced it fervently, treating it as a sacred duty, others were Muslims in name. I recall uncles who rarely attended mosques, except for special occasions such as weddings, naming ceremonies, or housewarming events, where they sought blessings through Islamic prayers. On some occasions, mosque leaders declined invitations from such uncles, citing their lack of financial contributions or poor attendance, particularly at Friday Jum'ah prayers. However, these refusals were often reversed when financial donations were made, a practice that revealed the intersection of religion and socio-economic dynamics.

The villages of Ago-Iwoye were numerous, and their populations were shaped by the willingness of family members to maintain biological ties and safeguard their collective socio-economic interests. Some villages demonstrated economic and political initiative, establishing primary schools to serve not only their children but also those from neighbouring villages. These schools transformed their villages into pivotal community hubs where residents convened to address mutual interests, such as trading markets, security, and infrastructure development. Communal efforts also led to the establishment of secondary schools in some villages, reducing the need for children to commute to town weekly.

A common feature of village life in those days was the practice of children leaving for schools in town on Sunday afternoons and returning on Friday evenings. This arrangement provided them with a change of environment and a taste of independence, away from the constant supervision and domestic obligations imposed by their parents. For parents, it ensured their townhouses were occupied and maintained during the week, with essential tasks such as clearing weeds and repairing damages undertaken by the children. These houses, typically constructed with mud, required consistent upkeep to prevent erosion and structural collapse caused by heavy rainfall.

What was most spectacular was the unison among the schoolchildren and the way they cooperated and aligned when embarking on their first trip on Sunday from the village to the town. The fact that they lived as neighbours in both the village and the town fostered an unimaginable understanding among them.

Respect for seniority in terms of age was also clearly evident. Everyone knew their place in the age hierarchy. Under no circumstances would anyone dare to be confrontational, rude, or insulting to someone older, even by just a few months. This respect greatly facilitated the communal division of labour during their transitions between the village and the town, whether travelling on Sunday afternoon to begin the school week or returning on Friday afternoon after school had closed for the weekend.

The most enjoyable aspect of their trips was the adventurous spirit the boys adopted. If they treated the journey as a timed individual endeavour, it might take three hours. However, as a group, the same journey could stretch to eight hours as they jointly undertook the adventure. While their parents made adequate provisions for the five days they spent at school in the town, the boys preferred to embrace their independence once free of parental supervision. They eagerly anticipated the journeys and relished every moment with their peers.

Opportunities for such trips often arose during cocoa harvest season when my mother had to join my father in the village for agricultural work. Each wife was required to spend at least five consecutive days assisting her husband on the farm, whether harvesting cocoa pods, kola nuts, corn, yams, cassava, or other crops. Consequently, it became inevitable that I travelled with my mother or joined her in the village on such occasions.

The journeys might well be described as 'hunting expeditions.' The oldest in the group held authority over everyone else and their opinions. This senior member knew the strengths and backgrounds of the group, including which boys excelled at using catapults to kill squirrels, bush rats (called *Okete*), and even birds perched in trees. Those less skilled in hitting targets ventured roughly a mile and a half into the bush, shaking the vegetation to flush out animals and birds toward the more skilled hunters. The game caught during these hunts provided extra meat for their soups, whether in the town or back in the village.

In some cases, close familiarity between individuals or shared names necessitated a means of differentiation, often based on religion or age. For instance, two villages named Lagan were distinguished by their predominant religions: Lagan Onimale, populated by Muslim families, and Lagan Onigbagbo, inhabited by Christian communities. Geographical distance also played a role in naming villages. The nearer village might be called Lagan Akoko (the first Lagan), while the one farther from the town could be named Lagan Tiwaju (the Lagan ahead). Similarly, Yoruba traditions incorporated religious practices such as *Osugbo*, *Agemo*, *Egungun*, or *Oro* into village names, as in Agbole Olosugbo.

In some instances, the activities associated with a specific settlement influenced its name. I vividly remember a man, renowned for healing mentally ill patients (W*ere* or *Asinwin*), who was widely known as Dalemo. His fame attracted families from distant towns and villages to his hut for treatment. Since the healing process often took years, some families built their huts nearby to remain close to their relatives under his care. Over time, the settlement became known as Dalemo Village.

What was striking about Dalemo Village was the way its name came to symbolise abnormal conduct or behaviour. People exhibiting unusual character traits were often asked, 'Have you just escaped from Dalemo?'–implying they had fled treatment for mental ailments. Such remarks could provoke catastrophic repercussions. In some cases, families whose members were ridiculed in this manner retaliated with deadly violence, considering it a grave insult. Records even recount instances where individuals were murdered for such careless jokes, highlighting the societal weight of perceived character defamation.

CHAPTER THREE

THE COMPOSITION OF THE TOWN

As noted in Chapter One, Ago-Iwoye was geographically recognised as the fourth largest town in Ijebu-land, following Ijebu-Ode, Ijebu-Igbo, and Shagamu. It was formed through the convergence of approximately seven quarters, comprising different groups of people who were compelled by external wartime challenges to unite. This union was necessitated by the need to defend themselves against marauding, war-hungry, and aggressive communities, particularly from the Egba lands of Abeokuta.

Each of the seven quarters maintained its distinct cultures, religions, and traditions, including separate times for marking religious celebrations. This separation was carefully observed to avoid physical clashes during the observance of ancestral rites and customs. Within each quarter, there was a diversity of religious groups, including Christian denominations, Muslim sects, and traditional worshippers with varied practices.

Reaching a consensus that respected the different religious beliefs and practices of these groups must have been a herculean task. It likely involved lengthy conferences and extensive deliberations to establish agreements that all parties could honour and uphold.

The seven quarters in Ago-Iwoye, as I knew them while growing up, are as follows:

1. Isamuro
2. Ibipe
3. Idode
4. Igan
5. Odosinusi
6. Imere
7. Imosu

Ososi, officially recognised as a quarter approximately thirty years ago, was well known and highly conspicuous in the development of the town. Though it was only recently accorded quarters status–bringing the total number of quarters in the town to eight–it has played a significant role in the community's history. Otunba Nuberu was the first to be crowned as the Otunba of Ososi.

Although I do not possess any evidential documents to detail the agreements reached concerning Ososi's upgraded status, nor any verbally authenticated statements from reliable sources, such agreements in those days were often sacrosanct despite being unwritten. Cultural methods of sealing agreements included tasting each other's blood, jumping over a laid-down gun, or touching a cutlass with their tongues–rituals meant to ensure secrecy and commitment. These practices were designed to prevent betrayals or the dissemination of sensitive information to enemies, reinforcing the sanctity of the covenant.

One peculiarity that persists today is the agreement concerning the title of Otunba. This title, which was at one point altered to Baale, was eventually restored to its original form. The title rotates among recognised families within each quarter, ensuring that the position passes equitably among qualified lineages. In Yoruba tradition, it is not said that an Oba or Otunba has died; rather, it is stated that they have gone to join their forefathers. Upon the passing of an Otunba, the next ruling family nominates a candidate from among its members. This nominee must be approved by the other recognised families and subsequently presented to the Ebumawe, who confers the staff of office.

This rotational system is designed to prevent disputes among the ruling families. However, contemporary politics, coupled with the influence of wealth and other external factors, has sometimes disrupted these traditional processes, turning selection into an internal matter of contention.

The criteria for selecting a suitable candidate for Kingship or Otunbaship include wealth, education, contributions to development projects, and general popularity within the community. Any individual born to a male or female member of the next ruling family is eligible. The nominee's name is first submitted to the Oba of the town, who forwards it to the Awujale of Ijebu-Ode. The Awujale, in turn, sends the name to the state government for final approval and the coordination of the coronation ceremony, during which the staff of the office is presented.

Historically, the selection of candidates involved a consultative process with the Afobaje (the kingmakers) and the Onifa, a priest who uses the Opele to establish the will of the gods. The Opele, a string of beads resembling Muslim's Tasbih or Catholic's

Rosary Beads, was consulted to determine the most suitable candidate from a list provided by the kingmakers. The Ifa's decision was deemed final. The candidate whose name caused both faces of the Opele to land upwards was considered the chosen one.

Disputes over this process were not uncommon, and dissatisfied candidates often pursued their grievances through the courts. Despite such challenges, once installed and handed the staff of the office, an Otunba traditionally holds the position for life. Only in extraordinary circumstances might removal be considered, though this is rare and avoided to preserve peace, continuity, and tradition.

After the unprovoked and unplanned war by the Egba people referred to as 'Gbeleke', Ago-Iwoye suffered serious defeat and humiliation. An Egba entourage had been sent ahead to inform the Balogun of Ago-Iwoye of their intention to visit the town and participate in one of its annual festivals. While the people of Ago-Iwoye were busy preparing to entertain their anticipated guests, the latter had secretly armed themselves to the teeth, ready for a campaign of destruction.

Caught unawares and unprepared for conflict, the town was ambushed from all four major points. What had been envisioned as a joyous ceremony turned into an unanticipated war. The people of Ago-Iwoye were overrun, their town reduced to ashes, and their pride battered. However, they managed to escape with a few ornaments, which they later presented to the Colonial Supervisors as evidence of a beaded Oba once reigning in the town. This gesture facilitated the restoration of the Kingship title for the future continuation of the traditional leadership.

Before delving into the roles played by individuals, as recorded in history, it is pertinent to present Ago-Iwoye's remarkable historical contributions that elevated its standing in the former Western Region–politically, religiously, and culturally.

POLITICALLY

Ago-Iwoye was predominantly a one-party town. Although a small number of individuals aligned themselves with other political parties, the Action Group commanded the majority's loyalty. Those affiliated with opposing parties often refrained from voicing dissent publicly, fearing repercussions. Raising a flag or emblem of another party in front of one's house was considered perilous, potentially endangering both the individual and their family.

RELIGIOUSLY

The people of Ago-Iwoye demonstrated a remarkable tolerance for diverse religious practices. At a location called 'Ita Ale', meaning 'night market', various religions converged and found their roots. The central mosque, where Jumat services were held on Fridays, stood prominently in front of the Sango shrine. Likewise, the Agemo annual festival, deeply rooted in Ijebu culture, brought celebrants from across the region into town. Interestingly, their route passed through the premises of the first Muslim primary school before culminating in performances in front of the mosque. Notably, there were no clashes of dates or times for these religious events.

In 2024, I was informed that the Agemo ceremony took place on the 24th of August. However, there was no publicity surrounding the event. The lack of a local radio or television station deprived the ceremony of the attention it deserved. I was disheartened to realise that, although present in town on that day, I was unaware of the occasion. I hope enlightened individuals will produce pamphlets or other forms of public notices in the future. The annual festival promises to be a significant event, and I pray for support–perhaps from business sponsors or non-governmental organisations–to promote religious inclusivity and cultural heritage.

ORO FESTIVAL

The Oro festival was traditionally a nocturnal event, always preceded by weeks of public warnings. Women were strictly forbidden from witnessing the event, encapsulated in the saying: 'Wo fere, ko ku fere' (to see it is to die instantly). The Oro could also be invoked during times of impending disaster to protect the town. The timing of their activities was not fixed, as they served to maintain stability in response to threats or crises.

EGUNGUN

The Egungun festival featured masquerades dressed in elaborate regalia, accompanied by traditional drummers. They paraded the town, receiving monetary offerings from observers. Women particularly revered these masquerades, often using the occasion to pray for marital harmony, childbearing, or business success.

More on the Egungun ceremonies will be elaborated upon later in the book.

OLORISA FESTIVAL

My favourite childhood ceremony in the town was the Olorisa festival. Its permanent site, located at Okebute in the Idode quarter, was managed by Hassan Olorisa, the cult leader. His entire family–wives, children, and others–were integral to the ceremonies. Dancers, drummers, and singers mesmerised the audience. Although Hassan was born into a Muslim family, he claimed to have received a divine vision leading him to serve the god of Orisha.

The festival's seven-day anniversary attracted people from within and beyond the town, drawing no boundaries in terms of religion or social standing. Both young and old eagerly anticipated this annual event, a time of cultural pride and joy.

OSUGBO HOUSE

Every quarter of the town hosted an Osugbo house, regarded as the spiritual foundation of the community. Access was traditionally limited to the most senior male elders and strictly forbidden to women. Despite this restriction, I managed to enter during my younger days out of religious curiosity. Contrary to expectations, I found nothing that should inherently exclude women. The hall resembled modern-day event centres, featuring a stage for musical instruments and an open space for gatherings. Admittance for male children of my age group was permitted, and I relished the cooked meats with *ebe* (a traditional soup) served during ceremonies. The sight of men dancing bare-chested during anniversaries remains vivid in my memory.

CHAPTER FOUR
POLITICS IN AGO-IWOYE

Every human being in Ago-Iwoye is highly political. During the years when politics was deeply rooted at the grassroots level, the majority of the population were ardent supporters of the Action

DUNIA HOUSE

Group (AG), which dominated the early stages of political development. Criticism of the party or its leaders was unheard of, as they were revered almost as gods. Many individuals from Ago-Iwoye held prominent roles within the party hierarchy, alongside numerous enforcers of discipline. Anyone who went against the party or its prominent members was swiftly reprimanded.

The King of the town, Oba David Moloniti Osiyemi, was selected as a member of the House of Chiefs due to the active political loyalty of the citizens and his qualifications. Notably, he was the most educated among the Obas in the chamber, which earned him the prestigious position of Secretary of the House. His education, coupled with his stature within the ruling party, afforded him this notable role.

Another illustrious son of Ago-Iwoye was Chief Akin Oshuntoye, a figure who placed the town on the map of prominence. Highly respected within his age group and beyond, he was a pioneer in the construction of grand residential estates, even before Dr. Dojo Onabamiro introduced significant architectural advances. Chief Oshuntoye's residence opposite Wesley Primary School, Mososi, was the first compound in the town to feature iron gates, marking a shift in architectural sophistication. His second house, Dunian House at Igan, was a masterpiece of innovation, captivating onlookers with its unique two-storey design and curvilinear shape, making it a local tourist attraction.

Whenever Chief Oshuntoye visited the town from Ibadan, where he was based as a businessman, an atmosphere of excitement enveloped Ago-Iwoye. A distinct alarm, sounding at intervals, signalled his arrival–a practice unprecedented in Ijebu land. His annual birthday celebrations were grand events, spanning an entire week, complete with traditional music, dancing, and processions. Mounted on a white horse, he would parade the town's major quarters, acknowledging the joyful acclamations of his well-wishers. Members of his age group, 'Egberegbe', adorned in coordinated damask attire, would accompany him, while women sang and danced in honour of the occasion.

When the procession reached my family home in Okebute, Chief Oshuntoye would make a detour to pay homage to my father. Seated on his special reclining chair–a common feature among elders at the time–my father would receive him, surrounded by other family elders. In a display of respect, the horse would rear seven times before Chief Oshuntoye resumed his parade.

The town also produced fearless defenders of the Action Group during periods of political unrest and violence. One such individual was Dauda Odumuyiwa, popularly known as 'Dauda Tinko.' A staunch protector of the party leadership, he was a trusted driver for Chief Obafemi Awolowo. In times of chaos, Dauda Tinko served as both driver and security officer, ensuring the safety of Chief Awolowo from assassination attempts and violent clashes orchestrated by opposition parties.

Another figure of note was Mojeed Ogberegede, a similarly respected and feared ally of the Action Group. Recognised as a founding member of the *Operation Wet ẹ*[1] movement during the violent clashes between 1962 and 1965, his loyalty and bravery

---

1 The phrase 'Operation Wet ẹ' originated from the act of dousing politicians and their properties in petrol and setting them on fire. Many victims of this political violence were killed through 'necklacing.' In the early 1960s, Nigeria experienced a surge in political violence, prompting the initiation of Operation Wetie, where political gangs were deployed to disrupt elections.

were legendary. Though little is known about his aliases, his strategic role during this turbulent period remains a significant part of Ago-Iwoye's history.

There was also a young boy, no more than seven years old, nicknamed 'Ajami Roku', who was believed to test the efficacy of traditional charms and medicines during the *Wet ẹ* era. Stories about him were extraordinary–claiming, for instance, that touching an enemy's house with his back would result in its destruction or that he could withstand being pounded in a mortar without harm. These accounts, while mythical, reflect the widespread belief in traditional powers at the time.

The loyalty of Ago-Iwoye to the ruling party was eventually rewarded by Governor Olabisi Onabanjo, who established Ogun State University (OSU) in the town. Now renamed Olabisi Onabanjo University in his honour, the institution has significantly contributed to the town's economic and infrastructural development. Visitors to its campuses appreciate the legacy of Chief Onabanjo, whose contributions remain deeply cherished. May his soul rest in peace, and may his family continue to receive the goodwill of Ago-Iwoye's people.

Another distinguished son of Ago-Iwoye was Chief Titi Solaru, father of Barrister Banjo Solaru. Chief Solaru served as the first chairman of Western Nigeria Television (WNTV), Africa's first television station, and later as chairman of Nigeria Airways Limited. His entrepreneurial ventures included ownership of the Oxford University Press in Apapa, Lagos, marking him as a notable figure in the annals of the town's history.

Jubril Martin Kuye was a renowned industrialist, a university student activist, and a politician who rose to the esteemed position of Federal Minister. During his time at the University of Ibadan, he was among the delegates sponsored by the Nigerian government to advocate to institutions, governments, and investors in the United Kingdom that the Biafran War was not an act of genocide but a familial misunderstanding, the resolution of which necessitated a civil war.

After completing his studies, he ventured into the paper production industry by establishing Pyramid Papers, achieving remarkable success in the sector. Notably, former President and one-time Military Head of State, Chief Olusegun Obasanjo, acknowledged in his writings and public lectures that it was Jubril Martin Kuye who first approached him, insisting that he was the most suitable candidate to become Nigeria's first democratic president. This recommendation preceded the 1999 election that marked Nigeria's transition to democracy. Kuye supported Obasanjo's candidacy during the campaigns, and after Obasanjo's victory, he was appointed Minister in the Federal Ministry of Finance.

As a philanthropist, Kuye contributed significantly to the development of Olabisi Onabanjo University, donating funds, equipment, and materials for infrastructural advancement. The people of Ago-Iwoye remember his generosity, and prayers are offered for his eternal peace in the afterlife. Insha Allah, may heaven grant him a place in paradise.

Another prominent political figure from Ago-Iwoye is Adesegun Abdel-Majid Adekoya. A native of the town, he currently serves as a member of the Federal House of Representatives in Abuja, representing the Ijebu North/Ijebu East/Ogun Waterside Federal Constituency. As a member of the People's Democratic

Party (PDP) and the party's National Executive Council, he has made significant contributions, particularly in improving road infrastructure, drainage systems, and other developmental projects too numerous to list.

Equally noteworthy is the biologist and statesman who conducted groundbreaking research on the devastating guinea worm disease that plagued southwestern Nigeria in the 1940s and 1950s. His discovery identified the cause of the disease as *Cyclops*, which was later named *Tropocyclops onabamiroid* in his honour. Beyond his scientific achievements, he played a pivotal political role, coining what is now known as the 'Tactical Committee', a strategy employed by Chief Obafemi Awolowo to navigate political meetings effectively.

He also served as the Western Region's Minister of Education, overseeing the establishment of the prestigious Obafemi Awolowo University in Ile-Ife and implementing the region's free education programme. As Secretary of the Universities Council, he remained instrumental in education until his passing. His burial service, held at the Methodist Church in Oke-Ita, was attended by Major General Oladipo Diya, who represented the Federal Government while serving as Vice President under General Abacha.

Ago-Iwoye is home to numerous individuals who have excelled in their professions and careers, contributing to the town's legacy. As this book progresses, we may revisit and highlight additional distinguished personalities who have made their mark.

CHAPTER FIVE

THE KINGSHIP OF AGO-IWOYE

Every town in Yorubaland traditionally had a head who was the first citizen of the town. This position was once regarded as sacred, and as such, it was not open to ordinary individuals. While the English term for this role is 'King', the equivalent in Yorubaland is referred to as *Oba* (meaning 'beaded head'). Wherever an Oba went, he was saluted and honoured with men prostrating and women kneeling as a gesture of respect, accompanied by the salutation 'Kabiyesi o o', meaning 'you are unquestionable.' Even those older than the Oba in age would bow to him as a mark of dignity. This underscored the gravity of the role–whatever the Oba declared, whether right or wrong, stood as the final word in any matter. The Oba was, in essence, the first citizen of his domain, much like a governor is the first citizen of their state or the president the first citizen of their country.

Historically, the process of selecting an Oba was rigorous and steeped in tradition. In those days, this process was strictly controlled by custodians of culture, unlike today, where modern political influences have started to encroach upon these sacred traditions. Every town and village had a council of elders, holders of traditional and chieftaincy titles, who were deeply knowledgeable about the history and traditions of their domain. This council undertook the solemn duty of identifying the family or quarter next in line to ascend the throne whenever an Oba passed away.

The process of Kingship followed a rotational principle among royal families or quarters. When the time came for a particular family, any eligible male child from that lineage could express his interest in being selected. Over time, societal changes have influenced these traditions. For instance, male descendants of women born into royal families–once excluded–can now vie for the throne, as exemplified by the story of Oba Sijuwade Olubuse of Ile-Ife, whose mother was a royal.

The kingmakers played a pivotal role, employing their experience and setting criteria to narrow down the list of candidates. Key factors included seniority, educational attainment, professional status, social contributions to the community, and past accessibility to the people. In the final stage, the *Ifa* oracle was consulted to eliminate doubts and ensure impartiality. This public consultation involved an oracle priest casting the *Opele* (divination chain) to determine the candidate favoured by divine will. The name of the chosen candidate was then announced, and a timetable for coronation rites was established.

Once selected, the candidate was secluded in a hut outside the town for seven days. During this period, he underwent traditional rites while receiving visits from well-wishers. Following this preparation, an official coronation ceremony took place, during which the new Oba was crowned and handed the staff of office–often by the state governor in the case of prominent towns. For lesser roles, senior Obas, such as the Awujale of Ijebuland or the Alake of Egbaland, officiated.

Culturally, women were historically excluded from ascending to the throne due to the secretive nature of some rituals. Certain areas within the palace and practices, like the *Oro* festival, were strictly off-limits to women. However, societal shifts have seen changes in this dynamic, allowing male descendants of royal women to claim the throne in their maternal towns, as seen with Oba Tejuosho, the Oshile of Oke Ona, Egbaland.

The death of an Oba referred to as 'joining the ancestors' (*Oba wo àjà*), was traditionally met with solemn rituals. Townsfolk would minimise social activities, especially at night, as sacrifices were often made as part of the burial rites. The practice of *Abobaku*–a person assigned to die with the Oba–was one such tradition, although it has largely been abandoned due to modern legal and social reforms. Nonetheless, much of the burial process remains steeped in secrecy, even when public religious rites such as Christian or Muslim services are conducted.

While the traditions surrounding the Kingship have evolved over time due to modernisation and religious influences, the essential cultural significance of the position continues to underscore the unique heritage of Yorubaland.

Let us direct our attention to the lineage of the Ebumawe of Ago-Iwoye ancestry, as that is the subject of this discourse. Where did the first person who established the right of kingship (Kingship) at Ago-Iwoye come from? Where did the individual who planted the seed of Kingship in the town originate?

History has it that, centuries ago in Ile-Ife, giving birth to and raising twins was strictly forbidden within the kingdom.[2] This prohibition extended to the Oba (King) of Ile-Ife himself. Having twin children was considered an abomination, and where such births occurred, the twins were removed from their family and sacrificed to the gods.

According to historians, one of the Oba's wives gave birth to twins–a boy and a girl. The Oba managed to keep this occurrence a closely guarded secret, known only to a select few among his trusted kingmakers. These confidants agreed with the Oba's decision to handle the situation covertly. Instead of following the custom of sacrificing the children, he devised a plan.

The Oba procured two baskets and filled them with materials that would enable them to float on a river. Each twin was placed inside a basket, adorned with royal symbols such as beads and other emblems of nobility. These baskets, containing the boy and the girl, were launched into the river under the cover of night.

As the river carried the baskets along its course, they drifted in different directions. The female child was eventually discovered in what is now the Ondo area, while the male child was found near the present-day Epe locality. As the boy grew up and began raising his own family, he faced challenges of acceptance within the community and eventually migrated to the current Ago-Iwoye township.

Those who found the twins were certain of their royal lineage, as evidenced by the ornaments and decorations in the baskets.

---

2 https://www.foluoyefeso.com/post/deconstructing-ibeji-twins-in-igbo-ora-oyo-state, https://shorturl.at/GduMx

However, an intriguing mystery remains: how did these children acquire the names by which they were known? Did the Oba of Ile-Ife leave written instructions in the baskets, or were the names inspired by the local communities? This remains a subject for further historical research.

The female child found in Ondo was named 'Osemawe', meaning 'mysterious one', while the male child discovered in Epe was named 'Ebumawe', meaning 'potent one.' In both names, 'Mawe' translates as 'here is' or 'here are.' Consequently, any Oba (king) of Ondo town from that lineage bears the title 'Osemawe', and any Oba of Ago-Iwoye must be a direct descendant of the prince from Ile-Ife and assumes the title 'Ebumawe.'

In Ago-Iwoye, the Kingship rotates among families from the seven quarters, and the final selection of an Oba is subject to approval by the town's kingmakers, following consultation with the Ifa Oracle. Once selected, the individual is crowned as Ebumawe. Each quarter has a head, known as an Otunba, who represents the Ebumawe and participates in palace meetings under the Ebumawe's chairmanship.

The Otunbas are tasked with presenting developmental issues and communal challenges at these meetings, ensuring collective contributions toward resolving such matters. Additionally, Otunbas and local chiefs are members of the Council of Chiefs in Ijebuland, led by the Awujale of Ijebuland.

Before an Otunba is formally installed by the Ebumawe, they must pay homage to the Awujale in Ijebu-Ode, receiving his blessings as a mark of approval and recognition. During town ceremonies, the Otunbas rally around the Ebumawe, supporting him physically, socially, and financially. This mutual cooperation fosters a harmonious community, as encapsulated in the Yoruba proverb: '*Osusu owo la fi ngbale*', meaning 'We use a bundle of brooms to sweep the floor.'

Historically, Ebumawe is recognised as a descendant of Oduduwa, the progenitor of the Yoruba people. The story of Oduduwa's offspring in terms of birth order and paternal affection remains a narrative for another discussion.

The male child, Akugbade, journeyed from Idoko to establish himself. Following the Egba war, remnants of the Iwoye people who escaped the conflict founded a settlement, referred to as 'Ago', under the leadership of Meleki, the Balogun (War Captain). The settlement's origins can be traced to the Imosi people.

The current quarters of Ago-Iwoye and their respective heads are as follows:

1. Ibipe - Ebumawe
2. Isamuro - Baruwa
3. Idode - Lewu
4. Odosinusi - Ayandelu
5. Igan - Mefu
6. Imosu - Sapenuwa
7. Imere - Obamowo
8. Oshosi - OluOshosi

The Ebumawe was reinstalled as Oba Ebumawe in 1944, as the second Ebumawe of the town, under the regnal name Fibigbade I 'Odo'. This took place in a designated area for conducting the preliminary rites preceding the coronation of a King or Baale. Let us now shift our focus to the relationship between the Osemawe of

WESLEY SCHOOL, IMOSOSI

Ondo and the Ebumawe of Ago-Iwoye, as well as the interactions between the people of Ondo and Ago-Iwoye as back as the 1950s.

In 1951, Oba Tewogboye, the Osemawe of Ondo, who reigned from 1942 to 1974, paid an official royal visit to his brother, Oba Oshinyemi, the Ebumawe of Ago-Iwoye. The occasion was marked by great pomp and regal splendour. I had the privilege of witnessing and participating in the welcoming ceremony as a schoolchild.

Despite the event occurring on a weekday, schools were closed in honour of the visiting royalty. Principals, teachers, and pupils lined the roads from the township's Oru Junction to Wesley School, Mososi, waving flags, singing, dancing, and clapping to a special welcoming song: 'Kabo o, Kabo, omo abile soro, omo abile soro, kile lanu kabo o' (Meaning: Welcome, welcome, the son of the soil who pronounced and the land opened, welcome.)

The townspeople enthusiastically joined the children in this celebration, showing their appreciation for the honoured guest. Markets and most shops were closed in deference to the royal visitor, regarded as the twin brother of their king. Oba Tewogboye was entertained at Wesley School premises, Mososi, in a manner reminiscent of the annual Empire Day events, before proceeding to the Ebumawe's palace. There is no record suggesting that the Ebumawe of Ago-Iwoye ever made a reciprocal visit to Ondo unless such a visit was carried out discreetly.

During the 40-year reign of Oba David Maloniti Oshinyemi as the Ebumawe, the town experienced two significant riots. The origins of these incidents remain speculative and unverified. The first, called the 'Onikondo' riot of 1954, saw residents carrying woods, planks, and sticks, destroying properties belonging to the government. The unrest was reportedly spurred by a rumour that the Ebumawe had advised the Ijebu Council in Ijebu-Ode to commence tax collection from farmers. Another unsubstantiated claim suggested the riot resulted from neglect in the worship of Sango, whose spirit was said to have risen angrily, disrupting the town.

The second riot occurred in 1971, amid allegations of misappropriation of funds from Ago-Iwoye Secondary School, supposedly involving the Ebumawe. Though the allegations could not be substantiated, the turmoil compelled the monarch to flee the town, reportedly trekking through the bush to Mamu, a small nearby town, before boarding a vehicle to Ibadan, where he sought refuge until peace was restored months later.

The Ago-Iwoye people were among the earliest communities to adopt age-group categorisation, with a three-year gap between groups. This tradition, dating back to the 16th century, fostered camaraderie among individuals born within a specific period in a given quarter who considered each other as siblings. These groups convened for monthly meetings, called 'Gbara', where they discussed and undertook community development tasks. Members failing to participate in assigned duties faced public reprimands or penalties authorised by the Oba.

A memorable example involved a wealthy, arrogant man who avoided his age group's meetings and opted instead to associate with a senior age group. Despite repeated warnings, he remained defiant. His peers resorted to public shaming, often congregating at his residence after completing communal assignments, publicly disgracing him before his neighbours. On some occasions, they seized robust sheep belonging to the absentees, announcing that owners could collect payment from the defiant members. My mother, possessing many sheep, frequently endured such seizures but never sought compensation, considering it her contribution to good neighbourliness.

Credit must be given to His Royal Majesty, Oba Abdul Rasaq Adenuga, the Okokodana Meji II, who successfully restored the age-group tradition to its historic prominence during his reign. The nomenclature of age groups, which had been dormant for years, was revived during the 2019 festival marking his coronation. The newly renamed cadre of *Egberegbe*, as popularly known, includes the following individuals:

1. Bobakeye   1956-1958
2. Gbobaniyi 1962-1964
3. Bobagunte 1964-1967
4. Arobayo   1968-1970
5. Tobalase   1971-1973
6. Obayori   1977-1979

The naming of the age group is often a grand event, characterised by elaborate fanfare, as both men and women in the group gather in their finest attire. They are supported by both senior and junior age groups, coming together to celebrate the milestone and special occasion. Musicians are frequently hired to entertain the guests, drawing both families and friends onto the dance floor, while money is sprayed onto the celebrants in a show of joy and admiration.

CHAPTER SIX

FORCED MARRIAGE IN AGO-IWOYE

I witnessed numerous incidents while growing up in Ago-Iwoye, transitioning from childhood to adulthood. These were not tales relayed through gossip or rumours, but events I personally observed. To readers from modern generations, the accounts

THE OLD MAGISTRATE COURT

may seem unbelievable, fabricated, or akin to fictions. But believe me, they were real. I played no role in creating these events, as they involved individuals significantly older than me and were resolved by our fathers' generation.

Life, as ever, is like a wind that blows unpredictably–from west to east, north to south–then suddenly reverses its course within moments. The cause of the wind's direction at any given time lies entirely outside human control. Even meteorological forecasts can predict what might occur but cannot explain why it happens or who causes it to happen. This is where the notion of the Creator of all things arises.

Wind, in its essence, is the natural movement of air or gases relative to a planet's surface. It occurs on varying scales, from thunderstorm flows lasting mere minutes to local breezes generated by land heating, which may last for a few hours. In much the same way, human life is unpredictable. Some are born in perfect health, yet illness or disability may later arise for one reason or another. Conversely, some are born with health challenges but, through modern medicine, medical tests, and regular care, become healthy over time. Such is the nature of life.

The Bible tells us that Jesus, the Son of God, once healed a crippled man who had been by the riverside for over 38 years, begging for alms. As Jesus passed by, their eyes met. Jesus, sensing the man's need, did not give him money. Instead, He asked the man to believe and have faith. The man professed his belief, and Jesus instructed him to stand and walk. From that moment, the man was healed and began walking.

The incidents I am about to recount were not second-hand stories, as such accounts can be inaccurate, exaggerated, or even entirely false. These, however, I witnessed with my eyes. Though I was not directly involved, I can name some of the key individuals who led the acrimonies that almost turned the town of Ago-Iwoye upside down. It was a traumatic period for parents, especially the mothers and fathers of young women.

Imagine, as a mother, sending your daughter on an errand–perhaps to sell wares or deliver a message. In those days, the freedom of movement seemed guaranteed by the natural order of habitation. But what if your daughter did not return home at the expected time, especially after dark? The worry would turn into anxiety, confusion, and eventual trauma, particularly if she had never stayed out late before and was known to be well-behaved.

There was a time when young girls were being kidnapped from the streets and forcibly taken to the homes of young men to become their wives. Sometimes, there might have been prior contact or a friendship between the girl and the man, but investigations often revealed no such relationship. Instead, the man–or sometimes an older man–simply admired the girl and acted on that desire. On several occasions, a man might try to court a lady and seek her favour, but if she rejected his advances, he might take drastic measures.

The next step for the man would be to approach a kingpin, a figure known in the community for engaging in illicit activities that had tarnished his name and reputation. Comparable to the street touts or garage figures of today, this kingpin had under his command a group of thugs or subordinates. Through prior arrangement, a contract would be established between the man and the kingpin. Following this, the kingpin would instruct his men to take the necessary actions upon receiving an advance payment.

The kingpin's associates would begin by monitoring the girl's movements–paying attention to where she frequented and whom she associated with. This surveillance, involving close observation, could last several days or even weeks before the eventual kidnapping was executed, with authorisation from the kingpin. The act of abduction involved forcibly taking the girl and delivering her to the house of the man who wished to marry her, bypassing the proper protocols of seeking parental blessings.

Once the girl was delivered to the man's house, akin to a parcel being dropped off, the contract terms with the kingpin were deemed fulfilled. What transpired thereafter became the sole responsibility of the prospective husband.

There were instances where the girl's family would not tolerate the forced marriage. In such cases, they would unequivocally demand that the man return the girl to her family home. This was often expressed in strong, uncompromising language. However, more frequently, the man would already have the support of his own family and close relatives, having convinced them to condone his actions. At this juncture, resolving the matter would shift towards negotiating with the girl's family through appeals, assurances, and, in some cases, compensation.

The man's family might plead with the girl's parents, promising to care for her, meet all her needs, and formalise the union by fulfilling cultural and traditional obligations, including the payment of dowry. On rare occasions, such overtures would earn the approval of the girl's family.

This is where the crucial role of mediators, often referred to as middlemen or middlewomen, came into play. These individuals, respected figures within the community, were tasked with preventing the dispute from escalating into open conflict between the two families. Acting on behalf of the man's family, they would begin by offering heartfelt apologies and expressing regret over the unfortunate turn of events.

In most cases, the girl's family, though initially incensed, would eventually relent, permitting the man's family to formalise the relationship through the requisite cultural practices. However, the mediator's task was fraught with risks. They could face hostility from the girl's family, who might accuse them of collusion with the kidnappers. It was a thankless assignment with no monetary reward–merely a duty that came with their status in the community.

My father was frequently called upon to mediate in such cases. I recall many occasions when families earnestly sought his intervention. He would begin by asking questions as though he were hearing the matter for the first time, deliberately withholding sympathy to maintain a neutral stance. Often, he would insist on speaking privately with the girl's father, as approaching the mother first risked provoking a dramatic outburst that could draw unwanted attention from the neighbours.

I was told of an incident where a girl's mother accused my father of siding with the kidnappers, even tearing his regalia in anger. Similarly, other mediators shared accounts of facing aggressive confrontations while attempting to broker peace.

In many cases, once the girl was delivered to the man's home, she was relocated to a relative's house in a distant area to avoid being traced or becoming the subject of gossip. Yet, there were instances where the girl's family discovered her location, prompting younger members of the family or community to organise a rescue mission. Such operations often escalated into violent confrontations, resulting in damaged property, injuries, and occasionally, bloodshed on both sides.

During that era, few of these incidents were brought to court. They were predominantly regarded as cultural issues and dealt with through traditional means. The police were seldom involved, as most families avoided filing formal complaints, preferring to resolve the matters within their communities.

Thank God, civilisation has ushered in a new and transformative dimension to the town, its communities, and its people. Consider, for instance, the significant number of Nigeria Police Force personnel now posted to the town, the numerous cases they handle, and the increased population when it comes to addressing incidents such as riots. The police force has been reinforced, both in numbers and authority, empowered by the Nigerian Constitution and judgements based on precedent cases to classify such acts as criminal offences punishable by up to ten years of imprisonment.

Previously, the police station was situated beside Wesley Primary School in Imososi. It has now been relocated to a larger, modernised site at Abobi, reflecting these infrastructural advancements. Similarly, the small Customary Court near Chief Akin Oshuntoye's compound, while still dispensing justice, has been complemented by the establishment of a larger, upgraded Magistrate Court now functioning near the Oba's palace.

Indeed, we are witnessing development as part of broader infrastructural progress.

CHAPTER SEVEN

CHILD HEAD INJECTION RUMOUR

Every town in Yorubaland has a unique characteristic that often ties to its historical foundation. These events, whether favourable or calamitous, caused by nature or human endeavour, are

CENTRAL MOSQUE, ITA

passed down through generations as part of the town's history or documented in records where such are maintained.

In the 1950s, during my primary school years at Ako Moslem School–located just behind the current site of the Central Mosque mentioned in earlier chapters–a singular yet catastrophic event occurred. It was a day whose repercussions left indelible marks on the spirits and mental health of many parents. In an instant, they envisioned their children being taken from them–not through illness, accidents, or natural disasters like volcanic eruptions or tsunamis–but by Colonial Masters, ostensibly under the guise of establishing civilisation, education, and Christianity for the children's future.

That day began like any other. Children attended their respective schools and, after the usual morning assembly and religious prayers, marched to their classrooms with rhythmic precision, their steps accompanied by the beat of 'gbam! gbam!! gbam!!!' They moved in orderly directions like soldiers, swinging their arms purposefully. Classes commenced as usual, and two lessons were underway when an uproar erupted outside the school.

Suddenly, a cacophony of distressed voices filled the air as multitudes of parents converged on the school, shouting the names of their children, and urging them to abandon their studies and come out. The panic was not confined to our school but spread across all schools in the town, irrespective of religious or geographical distinctions.

Inside the classrooms, chaos ensued. Frightened children ran in confusion, first seeking places to hide and later scattering across the school grounds. Those who recognised their parents' voices tried to escape and find them, while others, uncertain of their parents' presence, were paralysed by fear. Some children, particularly those whose families lived in surrounding villages and were only in town for school, faced the added uncertainty of returning home without fully understanding what was happening.

The situation overwhelmed the teachers and headmasters, who were equally clueless about the source of the pandemonium. How could they calm children who believed their lives were in imminent danger? A rumour had spread that half the children in certain schools had been killed, and their school might be next. The confusion was total; even the word 'chaos' seems inadequate to describe the disorder. The teachers had no choice but to support the children however they could.

At schools with gated premises, desperate parents broke down the gates. Men used sheer force, while women tugged at the gates until they yielded. Outside, parents shouted for their children, and from inside, the children screamed back for their mothers and fathers.

Within an hour, the serene township of Ago-Iwoye was transformed into a scene reminiscent of a warzone under invasion. Streets swarmed with frantic parents and guardians, some colliding violently without offering apologies, so consumed were they with locating their children.

What caused this confusion? A rumour, as explosive and destructive as an unanticipated volcanic eruption, spread without any reliable source of verification. In a time before the conveniences of modern technology–radio, television, or the internet–there was no way to confirm or debunk such alarming news. The rumour alleged that Colonial Masters based in Ijebu-Ode had resolved to kill schoolchildren across Ijebu land by injecting them with a deadly substance. According to the rumour, the children would die 12 hours after being injected, the plan having supposedly commenced in Ijebu-Ode and set to continue in Ago-Iwoye.

How did this rumour originate? It was later discovered that the entire story stemmed from a drunken remark made in a beer parlour in Ijebu-Ode. Two men, amid their revelry, concocted the idea. One, heavily inebriated, claimed he could cause widespread panic in Ijebu and detailed his method to his companion: he would board a bus to Ago-Iwoye, feign distress, and spread a false tale about children being injected by Colonial Officials. When the bus reached its destination, he dramatically announced his fabricated warning, prompting panic among his fellow passengers. As the passengers disembarked, they carried the baseless rumour into the community, where it spread like wildfire.

Thankfully, the Ago-Iwoye of today is far more advanced and would not fall prey to such primitive tactics of misinformation. Modern technology and the Nigeria Police Force, equipped with advanced tools, ensure that such upheaval would be swiftly quelled.

This account serves as a reminder to future generations and leaders of the kinds of challenges faced by their forebears. Despite the upheaval, it is worth noting that no deaths or serious injuries occurred. The few minor bruises sustained were mainly the result of collisions and falls during the pandemonium. At the time, the town's roads were untarred and muddy, a stark contrast to the modern infrastructure we enjoy today.

CHAPTER EIGHT
CHILDREN'S FUN MOMENTS

Ago-Iwoye was a very peaceful town in the 1950s, largely because we virtually knew everyone's family. The children attended primary school together and also gathered for Arabic lessons, known as *Ile Kewu*, after school hours from 16:00pm. to 18:00pm. Outside these periods, while there were unfortunate instances where young ladies were kidnapped into forced marriages, the younger generation enjoyed significant freedom of movement and association. Most of our parents were farmers who spent weeks or months in the village tending their crops, while the women stayed behind to assist in harvesting agricultural produce. This often meant that family houses in the town remained empty except during age-group meetings or other monthly gatherings, locally referred to as *Eregberegbe*. These meetings were a vital part of our parents' social lives, contributing significantly to the development of the town.

Children were required to attend school in the town from Monday to Friday. To ensure safety, groups of children left the village on Sunday afternoons and travelled together with others from nearby villages. This was to avoid being late on Monday morning, as tardiness could result in six lashes on the back or bottom. At that time, in the 1950s, latecomers were often held aloft by four strong boys–two holding their hands and two their legs–so the teacher could deliver the six strokes of punishment.

During these journeys, children developed the habit of hunting birds, bush rats, and squirrels (*Okere*) along the way. They would prepare these animals by smoking them over a fire and sharing them equally. This experience fostered communal togetherness and served as an additional source of sustenance for the week. However, the activity had its risks. Encounters with snakes, which sometimes resulted in bites, were particularly dangerous. Some children learned incantations to counteract snake bites, aiming to prevent serious consequences.

The people of Ago-Iwoye valued their extended families, often buying acres of land and dividing them among siblings and children to build houses close together. For instance, my family–Ato Baale–had a large compound where many houses were built by the same lineage. This arrangement facilitated close contact during emergencies and reduced the need for long journeys to check on relatives.

Children often stayed with uncles or cousins in instances where their parents were unavailable. In my father's house, for example, we could be ten or more children from different families sleeping in the parlour–the living room where guests were entertained during the day. We slept on mats woven by skilled artisans and purchased at local markets. At night, we often shared stories about school, our travels, or our meals, albeit in hushed tones to avoid being overheard by adults. If our parents caught wind of any mischief, the offending child would be chastised and warned never to repeat such behaviour. This form of extended family care meant that parenting was a collective responsibility, encompassing both biological and related children.

Trust among families was strong, and it was common to entrust a child to a brother or neighbour, knowing they would treat the child as their own. Children received praise for good behaviour and discipline for offences, and they dared not report such punishment to their parents. To do so would only result in further reprimand for disgracing the family.

After school, some children were required to attend Islamic lessons, where punctuality was strictly enforced. Failing to attend or arriving late often led to punishment, such as being struck on the palms with a stick–typically three or six lashes based on the severity of the offence.

Children from non-Islamic families were free to play after school, engaging in activities such as football, which sometimes caused problems. Matches held in house frontages or on roads often led to accidents, like hitting unsuspecting passers-by. Offenders were frequently reported to their parents and punished, often by being made to kneel as a form of discipline. Boys also amused themselves by using catapults to hunt birds or aim at lizards perched on walls. This relentless activity even caused the lizards to flee at the sight of children.

Though the games and mischief had their consequences, they created lasting memories and taught us lessons about communal living and shared responsibility, shaping the foundation of life in Ago-Iwoye during the 1950s.

CHAPTER NINE

YOUTHS' NIGHT HANGOUT

Life ought to be enjoyed, and communities of shared interests should be nurtured. The activities you engage in as a toddler and the relationships you form at a young age may influence your middle years and develop into sibling-like bonds in old age. Ago-Iwoye in the 1950s was renowned for many elements that significantly impacted the youth of that generation.

During this period, some young people and middle-aged individuals could not advance their education beyond the free primary education provided by Chief Obafemi Awolowo during his tenure as Premier of the Western Region. For various reasons–often due to parental financial constraints–they were unable to proceed to modern school, which served as a preparatory step towards a teaching career. Despite their academic brilliance, intelligence, and eagerness to learn, the requirement to pay school fees barred many from sitting examinations or continuing their education.

Fortunately, Chief Awolowo's introduction of Africa's first free primary school education programme became a lifeline for numerous children. Supervised meticulously by Professor Sanya Dojo Onabamiro, this laudable initiative ensured many children could access education, enabling their potential and intelligence to flourish. Without it, many of today's notable political and professional figures in Nigeria might not have achieved their successes. May Chief Awolowo's gentle soul rest in perfect peace.

For those unable to further their formal education due to financial constraints, alternative paths were explored to secure a brighter future. At the time, tailoring was traditionally considered an occupation for older individuals who specialised in sewing the classic Buba and Sokoto attire, with occasional forays into Agbada regalia. However, when younger people entered the trade, they revolutionised it, introducing innovative designs and embellishments.

Others ventured into selling musical records, cartridges, and video cassettes. These young entrepreneurs also redefined the tailoring business by establishing roadside shops, making their trade more visible and accessible. Customers could admire the latest styles displayed in show windows while passing by. These shops often played popular music, uplifting the spirits of passersby and neighbours, and offering a backdrop for informal social gatherings.

This musical atmosphere was enriched by the works of renowned icons such as Chief Ebenezer Obey, King Sunny Ade, I.K. Dairo, Haruna Ishola, Ligali Mukaiba, and Yussuff Olatunji. These tailors transformed their profession into a hub of activity, where youths gathered at night to dance to Juju, Apala, and Sharaka music, often accompanied by the flashing lights of elaborate loudspeakers mounted outside their shops.

Notable among these entrepreneurs was Mr. Oshunneye, popularly known as 'Nagode', who set up shop near Wesley Primary School in Ishamuro Quarter, close to the government public well

(Idi Konga). His shop was a cultural epicentre, attracting young people with the latest musical records. During my visit to the town in September 2024, I noted, with some regret, that this historic school had been relocated. Nagode came from a reputable family, including Chief Oshunneye, a distinguished educationist.

Music played at these shops included classics from:

1. Chief Herbert Ogunde: *Eba mi bi agba iya lere o, Eba mi bi agba iya lere*.
2. I.K. Dairo: *Salome, Mo sori re o, Ise aje logbe mi de lehi o*, and others.
3. Tunde Nightingale (alias *Original Owambe*): *Omo abi lowo tun owo se, Tiwa lo lere, Ono moto, Na Poor-A-Poor*, etc.
4. Ayinde Bakare: *Eko Akete ilu ogbon, Igi da eiye fo*, etc.
5. Kayode Fashola: *Oba to mohun gbogbo, Bi pepoeye ba jokuta*, etc.
6. Chief Ebenezer Obey: *Iwai ka kope ara mi, Amaisiko londamu eda o, Alowo ma jaiye, Edumare so oro mi daya*, etc.
7. King Sunny Ade: *Esu biribiri ebo mi o, Ekilo fun omo ode, Nibi lekeleke gbe nfoso*, etc.
8. Ayinde Barrister: *Oke agba, Ao fi ye won pe soja loni ijoba*, etc.
9. Alhaji Haruna Ishola (*Baba Ngani agba*): *Oroki social club nilu Oshogbo, Soyoyo*, etc.
10. Yussuff Olatunji: *Asha nba eiyele sere, Egbe gbobe niyi Odogbolu*, etc.

Another key hub was located at Ita Kekere, at the junction where Idode Road, Igan Road, and Ibipe Road intersected. The shop, operated by a younger tailor, similarly attracted youth for evening dances. Congregations typically began around 5:30pm. and ended by 10:00pm., ensuring attendees could safely return home before the streets became unsafe due to robbers lurking in the darkness. While night guards patrolled between 11:00pm. and 5:00am., anyone caught outside their home risked severe penalties.

Social gatherings at venues like Kawonishe Bar near Wesley Primary School in Ota provided additional opportunities for interaction. However, socialising required caution, particularly in navigating relationships with adventurous young women, as certain associations could attract trouble from territorial socialites or their protectors.

Though perceived as innocent youthful engagement, these gatherings offered valuable avenues for networking, learning, and developing interpersonal skills. Such vibrant experiences defined the social fabric of Ago-Iwoye in the 1950s and remain a fond memory of that era.

CHAPTER TEN

GOVERNMENT'S WELL (IDI KONGA) ISHAMURO

The people of Ago-Iwoye owe gratitude to the colonial officials stationed in Ijebu-Ode, who, despite being based there, visited the town whenever issues required investigation. The residents

IDI KONGA ISHAMURO, 1944

of Ago-Iwoye were known for their intolerance of abuse or humiliation from outsiders. Once provoked, their tempers often led to significant damage to property and serious injuries to others.

The town was surrounded by numerous rivers, which served as the primary source of drinking water for its people. These rivers also provided opportunities for washing clothes, swimming lessons for the youth, and fishing. However, since these rivers originated far away, it was undeniable that at certain points along their course, they might be used for unhygienic purposes, including defecation. Consequently, the water's use varied at different points along the river's flow. Some residents resorted to digging deep wells beside the river, covering the tops with palm branches, and selling the water as safe drinking water.

Despite these measures, the town faced a devastating guinea worm pandemic. The disease disabled many people, leaving some unable to stand or walk without assistance and prematurely claiming thousands of lives. Many became crippled, and the burden of the disease stretched beyond the capacity of traditional herbal medicine to manage effectively.

In a bid to identify the source of the outbreak and provide a solution, colonial officials observed that the flowing river–the main source of drinking water–was likely responsible for the disease. To mitigate its spread, a decision was made to dig a deep well at the town's centre, located geographically between the Ishamuro and Imosun quarters. This location ensured no single quarter could claim ownership. The well was freely accessible to all residents to reduce reliance on river water and curtail the disease.

Guinea worm disease brought severe physical and economic suffering. For the infected, the condition began with intense itching on the legs, followed by swelling. Over time, the swollen area would burst, releasing a white liquid, and a long, thin parasite would slowly emerge. This process, often lasting weeks, was excruciatingly painful. Attempts to forcefully extract the worm could cause it to break, leading to reinfection. In some cases, multiple infections occurred simultaneously, significantly worsening the ordeal. Victims often isolated themselves due to the stigma associated with the disease, as it was mistakenly believed to be contagious.

Though the town had a single dispensary clinic located near where Ebumawe's Palace now stands, it lacked effective medication to prevent the disease. The clinic could only provide cleaning and basic treatment to accelerate the worm's emergence. Many residents turned to local herbalists, whose remedies were believed to expedite the process.

The disease drew the attention of Dr. Dojo Sanya Onabamiro, an esteemed researcher from Ago-Iwoye. His groundbreaking work on the intermediate host, cyclopid copepods, gained international recognition. His research, which identified the link between the parasite and water sources, earned him global acclaim and highlighted his hometown on the world stage. Onabamiro's findings were pivotal in addressing the guinea worm crisis and were commemorated in scientific nomenclature with the terms *Onabamiroi* and *Agoiwoyensis*.

Rumours surrounding the construction of the deep well–nicknamed 'Idi Konga'–further added to its lore. Some claimed that the diggers reported hearing voices from beneath the ground, supposedly from another world where the people spoke Yoruba and complained about dirt falling onto their homes and food.

While this anecdote could not be substantiated, it became a point of intrigue and amusement.

Ago-Iwoye has always been a town of high principles, moral justice, and a deep appreciation for education. As Kenneth Mellanby, the first principal of the University College Ibadan, remarked, the town's achievements in education were unparalleled. He specifically celebrated Dr. Onabamiro, whose work under his supervision brought prestige to the college and Ago-Iwoye alike.

In my youth, life in Ago-Iwoye was both challenging and filled with simple joys. One cherished pastime was playing in the rain. Whether light or torrential, the rain brought immense delight. The water would create eroding streams, sometimes strong enough to carry chickens away, and we turned it into a competition, running from house to house through the currents. Remarkably, we never fell ill from these adventures. Rainwater, often considered the purest, was favoured by the community as a hygienic source of drinking water.

CHAPTER ELEVEN

THE SOCIAL PARTY PEOPLE

The people of Ago-Iwoye are well known for celebrating occasions in grand style. Many visitors from other towns, states, and locations have been drawn to the town on invitations from friends, colleagues, neighbours, and online acquaintances, to attend significant events hosted by their relatives.

AKO MOSLEM SCHOOL, AGO IWOYE

In the 1950s, the Ako Moslem School, located behind the Central Mosque, was a renowned hub where townspeople gathered to enjoy performances by national and international musicians. These artists showcased their musical talents to entertain audiences who danced the night away. Remarkably, the musicians were not invited by individuals to perform as part of private celebrations but organised their performances independently, recognising the town's reputation for appreciating fine music. Entry fees were charged at the gate, ensuring controlled access to the hall. Consequently, these events were neither free-for-all nor places where one could freely exit and re-enter without regulation.

Despite efforts to maintain order, such gatherings were often marred by rowdiness. Disorder at the gates, caused by people trying to gain illegal entry without paying, frequently led to violent disruptions. Once violence broke out, attendees inside the hall were forced to flee for safety. What began as an evening of joy and music could quickly descend into chaos, with some individuals sustaining severe injuries. In extreme cases, injuries lead to lifelong disabilities. Efforts to maintain security were undermined by unruly elements that overwhelmed private, uniformed security personnel, whose presence at the time was not standard practice.

As a result, parents often forbade their children from attending such events, particularly during festive seasons like Christmas and New Year when these musical shows were most prevalent. Street parties and open-air events held on school grounds, such as Wesley Primary School at Imososi or Wesley Primary School at Ota, typically experienced fewer disruptions. These events, often hosted by identifiable individuals, provided a safer atmosphere where the town's reputation and the security of visitors were paramount.

Thankfully, the town has progressed significantly. The development of hotels and event centres with expansive halls has transformed how celebrations are organised. Celebrants can now book venues in advance, considering the hall's capacity before issuing invitations. These facilities employ uniformed security personnel, whose presence serves as a deterrent to troublemakers. Moreover, emergency contacts for the police and other relevant agencies are readily available, ensuring quick responses to any disturbances beyond the control of the hired security.

In August 2024, I visited Ago-Iwoye and was struck by the remarkable infrastructure, particularly along Olabisi Onabanjo Road, where the newly established and expanding WOSAM Event Centre caught my attention. Intrigued, I toured the centre's facilities, including accommodation for guests and entertainment halls tailored to varying budgets. I engaged in a detailed discussion with the duty manager, who graciously shared information about the centre's offerings. He mentioned that the 20th Coronation Anniversary of Oba Adenuga, the Ebumawe of Ago-Iwoye, had been celebrated at the venue earlier that year. This impressive establishment is a testament to the entrepreneurial spirit of its founders, who have enriched the town's landscape.

Traditional rulers in Yorubaland, such as the Ebumawe, play a vital role in ensuring peace and harmony in their domains. Ago-Iwoye benefits from a robust security network, which, although not organised by the Ogun State government, is effective in safeguarding the town. Combined with the efforts of the Nigerian

Police Force, regular patrols and community-sourced intelligence help maintain order.

For the town's continued progress, there is a need for a local media presence, including a radio and television station, to broadcast socially significant events. The Ebumawe once promised citizens living abroad that land would be made available for economic development—a commitment that should not waver. Broadcasting Friday Jumu'ah prayers and Sunday Christian services from various denominations could foster unity and showcase the town's spiritual activities. Festivals such as Egungun and Agemo should also be highlighted in advance to ensure greater participation.

As Ago-Iwoye embraces modernisation, it must celebrate and preserve its rich cultural heritage.

CHAPTER TWELVE

THE VILLAGE LIFE

The history of Ago-Iwoye cannot be comprehensively recounted or adequately presented to the citizens of the town or the wider world without acknowledging the life experiences in the farm villages, which served as the food baskets for the town and larger settlements, such as Ijebu-Ode, as well as more distant places like Ibadan and Lagos. People from other towns converged on the Ago-Iwoye market for trade, engaging in both buying and selling.

It is neither feasible nor practical to name every village associated with one quarter, such as Idode, let alone those belonging to the other eight quarters. However, the focus here is not on listing villages but on highlighting the lifestyle of the past. For instance, Idode, as a quarter, encompassed over twenty villages, including Ololo, which has now been incorporated into the main township of Idode and Ago-Iwoye. Each village in the 1950s was essentially a miniature town for its inhabitants, often established by specific families and named after their forefathers or ancestral lineage. Some villages had religious foundations; for example, in Idode, significant villages included Odosenlu and the two Lagans. Lagan Onigbagbo (Christian Lagan) was predominantly inhabited by Christians, while Lagan Oni-Male (Muslim Lagan), located further from the main road, was home to Muslim communities. Despite religious distinctions, people were generally free to live in any village, particularly if they had family connections or heritage ties there.

Most of our forefathers were farmers, though a few combined farming with trading in town. It was impractical to commute daily between the town and the villages due to the lack of adequate transportation. At that time, bicycles were a luxury, affordable only to the affluent, such as prosperous cocoa farmers. Motorcycles were rare, and their presence further underscored their owner's status and wealth. To simplify farm management and minimise travel, our ancestors established permanent residences in the villages. They built modest huts from mud, complete with wooden doors and windows for ventilation and privacy. Larger families necessitated more huts, creating small village communities.

Women played a vital role in supporting their husbands, particularly during harvest seasons, by gathering produce and transporting it to local markets, where they could purchase household necessities. Many women also engaged in small-scale commerce, selling items to neighbouring families and villages. Some even became processors, converting palm kernels into palm oil, cassava into gari, and other commodities.

Children born in these villages were often delivered without professional healthcare services, relying instead on traditional midwives. Emergencies occasionally required trips to hospitals in town, but such instances were rare. Families typically only returned to town for significant events, such as Christmas, New

Year celebrations, and Muslim festivals, or to attend familial, social, or age-group ceremonies.

The establishment of age-group societies, known as *Egberegbe*, was particularly noteworthy. Men and women of the same age formed associations, meeting monthly (*Gbara*) in town to address common concerns and contribute through financial support or manual labour. These groups were ceremoniously named by the reigning Oba, and their inauguration was celebrated with elaborate festivities.

Village life in those days, despite its simplicity, was filled with joy and camaraderie. Huts served as homes, and communal open spaces became venues for evening gatherings. Under the moonlight, we entertained ourselves, singing school hymns or traditional songs popularised by artists like Hubert Ogunde, I. K. Dairo, King Sunny Ade, and Ebenezer Obey. Children eagerly showcased their talents in music, drama, and dance, especially on Friday and Saturday nights, as these were their only free evenings.

Lagan Onigbagbo flourished, partly due to its early adoption of education through connections with the Wesley Christian denomination. By 1983, the village had established a primary school and later added a secondary school. In contrast, Lagan Oni-Male dwindled over time as farming became less appealing to younger generations, and the village was eventually abandoned. Many migrated to towns and cities, such as Ago-Iwoye, in search of crafts, trades, or careers to support their families.

For us schoolchildren, the weekly routine of trekking from the village to town on Sunday afternoons was both a necessity and an adventure. Carrying our washed school uniforms and foodstuffs in locally woven baskets, we enjoyed the freedom of being unsupervised by our parents. Along the way, we engaged in small hunting expeditions, catching squirrels, birds, and bush rats or collecting snails and mushrooms to enhance our meals. Fridays after school mirrored this routine, with added excursions to fish in nearby rivers or ponds.

Our time on the farms was not merely about assisting our parents; it was also a way to shield us from harmful influences and instil discipline. Parents closely monitored their children's behaviour to ensure they upheld family and community values. Both at home and school, we were taught to be role models for our families and to bring pride to our parents in their old age.

CHAPTER THIRTEEN

THE EIGHT QUARTERS OF AGO-IWOYE

Ago-Iwoye was originally made up of seven quarters. However, following a review of historical records and the contributions of some community leaders and other important personalities

CHIEF AKIN OSHUNTOYE'S HOUSE

(VIPs), an additional quarter was accorded royal status, similar to the existing seven. Imososi was traditionally recognised as a sub-entity of the Isamuro quarter, well known to locals and visitors alike. However, during the reign of HRM Adewale, concerted efforts were made, supported by historical evidence, to elevate Imososi to the status of an independent quarter. Once approval was granted, the quarter was designated an *Otunbaship*, assigning its royal head the title of *Otunba*. The inaugural Otunba of Imososi was the late Mr Nuberu, and the current Otunba, Professor Adebanjo (retired), is actively fostering peaceful coexistence in the quarter and the larger Ago-Iwoye township, while also ensuring the safety of its residents and their properties.

Imososi's rise to prominence has deep historical roots, though these are too numerous to document fully in this text. While historians possess richer records, only the most apparent aspects will be highlighted here. Since the establishment of Ago-Iwoye and the merger of its quarters into a cohesive township, the name 'Imososi' has often surfaced in discussions about the community. Despite its significance, Isamuro–acknowledged as the foremost and most influential quarter–historically overshadowed Imososi and delayed its rightful recognition. As human nature is inherently political, carving out a new quarter from an established one was met with resistance. Leaders feared being perceived as sell-outs or facing allegations of bribery. In a place like Ago-Iwoye, shaped by complex experiences, such suspicions could ignite speculation and unrest, including accusations of financial impropriety. As elders would caution, a riot resembles the fish *korowo*, which hears the command to leave but not to return.

For a long time, Imososi earned its renown through its association with individuals of high status who built expansive residences in the area. As the land was vast and largely undeveloped, affluent individuals could purchase sizeable plots, resulting in expansive compounds. Chief Akin Oshuntoye exemplified this trend by constructing a large house with additional structures for various purposes. His property included a spacious compound that could accommodate numerous vehicles securely and discreetly–an uncommon luxury at the time. Another prominent figure was Banjo Solaru, the son of Pa Titi Solaru, owner of Oxford University Press. Banjo, a lawyer by education, was also a celebrated radio broadcaster and a successful businessman. He acquired substantial land in Imososi, drawn by the peace and proximity to government institutions that the area offered.

Similarly, Otunba Shapenuwa, Otunba of Imosu, moved from his ancestral quarter in Imosu to establish a residence in the Idode quarter due to space constraints in his original domain. Despite the relocation, he continued to maintain strong ties with his community, frequently attending to their matters.

Notably, Imososi hosted the first police station in the town, making it a hub of daily activity as people reported incidents, and accidents, or sought assistance for community peace. This added to its prominence. Furthermore, the area was home to Wesley Primary School, which boasted the largest compound and playing field of all the schools in Ago-Iwoye. The school's grounds, lined with guava and orange trees, became a popular gathering place for children and adults alike. The fruits, freely available, fostered a spirit of shared community.

Wesley Primary School also served as the venue for major town events, such as the annual Empire Day celebrations, which highlighted Ago-Iwoye's connection to the British government and the Commonwealth. Events organised by civic groups, educational unions, and notable individuals also took place there. For example, the Ago-Iwoye Socialist Club once hosted an anniversary event on the school field, and a retirement celebration for Mrs Dehinsilu, a teacher, was organised by the teaching union on the same premises. The school became a training ground for many esteemed professionals, academics, and theologians.

Its inclusive policies allowed children from all religious backgrounds to enrol, and some students even transitioned from Islam to Christianity during their time at the school. For instance, Otunba Nathaniel Adegboyega Olusanya, originally named Nodiru, converted to Christianity and adopted a new name. Similarly, Lateef Soyombo became Zacchaeus Soyombo, and Folorunsho Olusanya became Festus Olusanya. Their decisions inspired other children, particularly from the Ato Baale family, to take similar steps, profoundly shaping their families' legacies.

CHAPTER FOURTEEN
VILLAGE VIBES AFTER DUSK

Life was very pleasant in the village during the 1940s, 1950s, and, to some extent, the 1960s. Adults often gathered beneath a well-branched tree, shaded by a canopy of banana leaves. These gatherings were inclusive and free from age or gender discrimination. It was a tradition that upon returning from the farm, one would first enter their hut and change into fresh attire, removing any odour or dirt acquired during the day. This practice ensured one appeared presentable and reflected the dignity of a true farmer, earning a living through honest labour.

People sat in an arrangement that corresponded to their age, as respect for seniority was deeply ingrained in the community. The elders, particularly those over seventy, were afforded special reclining chairs that allowed them to stretch comfortably. Some chairs featured extensions for resting their feet or placing their palm wine and calabash cups within easy reach. Palm wine, supplied in large kegs in its original, undiluted form, was a staple. However, inexperienced drinkers often found themselves overwhelmed after just a couple of cups.

The evening assemblies were a cherished tradition inherited from forefathers, and it was rare for anyone to miss them unless circumstances were unavoidable. These gatherings served multiple purposes. They were a hub for exchanging news, both local and from neighbouring villages. Issues affecting individuals or the community were discussed and resolved collectively. For instance, if there was a report of trespassing on someone's land, it would be brought to the attention of senior members, who would investigate the matter in advance. During the assembly, the findings would be presented, blame apportioned if necessary, and the dispute resolved amicably. Occasionally, more contentious matters arose, such as infidelity, which might require consulting a herbalist for spiritual guidance or practical remedies.

The herbalist played a significant role in village life, offering advice not only on personal issues but also on broader concerns, such as impending epidemics, poor harvests, or floods. He would prescribe rituals or actions to avert such crises, and the community would collectively decide how to implement these measures, including financial contributions or delegating responsibilities.

On special occasions, entertainers from nearby towns or villages were invited to perform. These events were accompanied by feasting, with various dishes prepared, allowing attendees to eat and drink to their satisfaction. Children under five were occasionally present, but older children and women typically did not participate in the men's assemblies. Instead, women held their gatherings, led by the most senior woman, known as the 'Iya Egbe', or 'head of the women.' These meetings focused on matters about the duties of wives and mothers. Women ensured they returned home well before their husbands to maintain domestic harmony.

School-aged boys and girls had their assemblies, particularly on moonlit nights, which lasted ten to fifteen days each month. These gatherings provided opportunities for the youth to share what they had learned in school, including songs, poems, and stories. Dancing often accompanied these meetings, showcasing both traditional and modern choreography. Not everyone excelled equally in singing or dancing, but standout performances, akin to those of King Sunny Ade on stage, often became the talk of the village. Occasionally, even the men abandoned their assemblies to witness the youths' creativity, drawing spectators from across the community, including women who took pride in the children's achievements.

The village, predominantly Muslim, observed a strong adherence to religious customs. It was customary for a wife to follow her husband's faith, and any deviation could lead to societal ridicule or even divorce. Despite the presence of various Muslim sects–such as Ahmadiyya, Ansar-ud-deen, and others–the community fostered unity. Different groups shared the same mosque for Friday prayers, demonstrating a spirit of harmony and mutual respect that I admired during my teenage years.

CHAPTER FIFTEEN

RELIGIOUS ACTIVITIES IN AGO-IWOYE

Let us be honest with ourselves, to ourselves, and each other. The Yoruba people and Yoruba land inherited their religions from their ancestors. No religion can claim superiority over another. All religions emerged for one purpose or another, and as long as that purpose is fulfilled, it must have the approval of the Lord, the Creator of the universe.

The primary challenge with Yoruba traditional religion is its lack of written records, development, innovation, and modernisation, which would make it more attractive to the youth and appealing to the wider populace. Additionally, there are sacrifices and ingredients deemed essential by those who served these gods, as prescribed by the elders, which were made compulsory to achieve the desired outcomes. These practices often hinder the religion's appeal in the face of evolving human endeavours.

I was a witness, and perhaps indirectly a participant, in many traditional religious practices while growing up in the township of Ago-Iwoye. Perhaps out of curiosity or due to my youthful instincts, I engaged in what my peers were involved in at the time. One area where foreign religions managed to overshadow and supplant our traditional religion and heritage was in their structured doctrines and global appeal. Modern philosophies might dismiss traditional practices, but the Yoruba possess a divine medium through which they serve God, protecting and blessing themselves, as seen in their ancestral traditions. These practices granted them the ability to protect their properties, acquire good health, enrich their lives, defend themselves, and implement justice in their societies.

History provides substantial evidence that the Yoruba race originated from somewhere in the present-day Middle East. Much like the Arabs, Jews, and Palestinians, who originated from the same region and have remained there, the Yoruba people's migration to their present land remains an enigma. No historical or religious text I have read explains what compelled the Yoruba to leave their ancestral land or the routes they took to reach present-day Yoruba land. Some time ago, the Awujale of Ijebu-land, Oba Sikiru Adetona, mentioned in an interview that the Ijebu people were referenced in the Holy Bible as the Jebusites. Interestingly, no historian or religious body has contested this statement. Prominent figures such as Adeboye, Oyedepo, and Suleman Johnson have also refrained from disputing the Awujale's assertion. Let us, for the sake of this discussion, assume the Awujale was correct.

If the Yoruba had been gifted with the ability and knowledge to document their religious practices and traditions, as the Christians and Muslims have done, perhaps their religion would have gained the honour and credibility it deserves. The differentiation between capitalised 'God' and lowercase 'god' about

African deities diminishes their perceived significance. The introduction of foreign practices, such as the abolition of human sacrifice by Mary Slessor, marked a significant turning point in the perception and practice of traditional worship. Such interventions led to the Europeanisation of African religious modes.

The arrival of the Arabs and their Islamic traditions in Yoruba life is worth critical examination. Separated from the Yoruba for thousands of years by differences in culture, religion, trade, and politics, the Arabs imposed their religious practices upon the region. Without apology, the Arabs' historical arrogance and belief in their superiority over other races, including blacks, shaped their interactions. Despite British and American classifications treating all as *black people*, the Arabs sought to establish dominance over their subjects, exploiting them economically and culturally.

The Arabs, as the first colonisers, initiated the trans-Saharan slave trade, chaining their captives and marching them across the desert. Their initial contact with West Africans was not for trade in commodities but for acquiring slaves for domestic and agricultural purposes. The Europeans, in contrast, transported slaves across the Atlantic. The Arabs' imposition of their religion followed the outlawing of the slave trade, whereas Christianity gained converts through education, persuasion, and support. Islam, by contrast, adopted a totalitarian approach, branding non-adherents as infidels and often subjecting them to severe punishment.

Why do we embrace Christianity or Islam today? The answer is evident in the historical trajectory of these religions, documented in texts such as the Bible and the Quran, which are used to educate future generations. While both texts claim divine inspiration, their authenticity lies in their ability to standardise and propagate faith. However, neither Jesus Christ nor Prophet Mohammed (peace be upon him) is explicitly credited with authoring these texts; their teachings were preserved and passed down by others. Faith, ultimately, is a matter of belief and adherence.

In Ago-Iwoye, all religions–both indigenous and foreign–coexist harmoniously. Despite differences in longevity, negotiation, or compromise, they maintain peace and tranquillity. The central square, Ita Ale, serves as a shared space for religious activities under structured agreements to avoid conflict. The Central Mosque, the House of the Osugbo, and the annual Alagemo festival exemplify the town's commendable religious tolerance.

May Ago-Iwoye continue to flourish in peace and harmony.

CHAPTER SIXTEEN
MOTHER'S ROLES

It is indisputable that, in the life of a child, at least one parent must have played a significant role in imparting training for the child's future. In some cases, the father assumes this role, sharing stories about his life, the family tree, and the community at large. In other instances, however, despite living in the same house, the father may be absent from the child's life. It is rare for both parents to play equally active roles in shaping a child's life. While the father is often regarded as the breadwinner, circumstances may prevent him from being physically present to mould the child's behaviour and guide their conduct for the future.

God, in His kindness and benevolence, blessed me with a mother whose parenting approach, though initially resented, turned out to be a cornerstone of my development. She restricted me from the kind of freedom that could lead to waywardness, as was evident in the lives of some of my childhood neighbours. When you are prevented from going out at will, playing football on the road like other children, returning home whenever you please, or watching masquerade displays during annual festivals, you may perceive yourself, by modern standards, as a slave within your home.

My childhood was as structured as modern computer data, even though there were no computers or mobile phones at the time. My upbringing under my mother was characterised by regimental orderliness. I recall sleeping on mats woven locally from straw, as my mother did not own a bed. Only my father had a wooden bed with a mattress filled not with wool but with leaves. Each morning, I had to wake early to complete my scheduled duties before going to school. These tasks were not forcefully imposed but were contributions I willingly made to the growth and harmony of the family under my mother's guidance.

At some point, circumstances in the family compelled me to view my mother as the head of one household and my father as the head of another, even though we lived under the same roof. God opened my eyes to see my mother's struggles to shape the future of her children. She sacrificed her youthful friendships and her membership in her age group, called *Egberegbe*, channelling all her energy and resources into raising us. Towards the end of her life, she did not regret the disciplinary measures she had employed, which had shaped us for the better.

My father, with his many wives and children, found it difficult to lead the charge in educating us through the Western system. I vividly recall attending Arabic lessons after my primary school hours. When I progressed to a level requiring the celebration of achievements–such as killing and cooking a chicken or, later, a goat–it was my mother who provided the necessary resources. By the time I reached the postgraduate level in Arabic studies, capable of translating between Arabic and Yoruba, the elaborate celebration typical of such an achievement was beyond our means. While some families could afford to buy a cow and hire traditional musicians, I had to scale down my aspirations to fit our modest resources, foregoing social extravagance.

My father, by nature and inclination, rarely shared stories or wisdom that could guide us in life. Fortunately, my mother filled this gap. Despite her demanding schedule, which stretched from 4 a.m. to 11 p.m., she found time to share stories and lessons she had learned from her mother or personal experiences. As an Arabic student, I was taught to disregard traditional worship and challenge the efficacy of gods without eyes, hands, or brains. However, my mother emphasised respect for all religions and beliefs, urging us to give Caesar what belongs to Caesar and God what belongs to God. She believed that respect and understanding were better than confrontation.

One of her lessons was about respecting elders. She recounted the story of a young man who mocked an elderly individual using a walking stick. When the young man refused to return the stick, he was cursed to laugh uncontrollably until his death–a cautionary tale about the consequences of disrespect. She also shared a story about the *Alagemos*, traditional worshippers who experienced a mishap during their annual festival. Their leader cursed a river to never rise beyond knee level, a curse that endures to this day.

Finally, my mother taught us the importance of history, stories, and experiences in shaping one's understanding of the world. She highlighted the balance between respecting traditions and embracing modernity, warning against arrogance and impulsiveness. These teachings have remained a vital part of my outlook on life.

History recounts what has occurred, stories convey imagination or second-hand knowledge, experience teaches lessons through personal encounters, and desire fuels hope for the future.

CHAPTER SEVENTEEN

THE ANNUAL TRADITIONAL FESTIVALS

There are numerous traditional and cultural ceremonies performed at Ago-Iwoye. While there are too many to list comprehensively, I will mention some notable ones and provide brief narratives about them:

THE SANGO HOUSE, ITA

1. The School Empire Day
2. The Egungun Festival
3. The Oro Festival
4. The Agemo Festival
5. The Oshugbo Festival
6. The Olorisa Festival
7. The Sango Festival
8. The Ojude Oba Festival
9. The Isese Festival
10. The Christian Festivals
11. The Muslim Festivals
12. The Orunken Festival

THE ROLE OF THE OBA IN RELIGIOUS AND CULTURAL CEREMONIES

For anyone chosen to ascend the coveted position of Oba Ebumawe of the town, regardless of their religious background–whether a devoted Apostle of a church or an Imam at a mosque–there is a requisite shift in approach. Such an individual must become flexible and embrace participation in all religious ceremonies and festivals, transcending personal or familial beliefs.

While the Oba is not compelled to renounce their faith, they must embody the role of a cultural and traditional father, serving as the head of all religious and cultural practices in the town. This neutrality ensures inclusivity and fosters peace. The Oba's physical presence at these ceremonies is paramount, symbolising unity, even if they are not required to partake in activities that contravene their religious doctrines.

This inclusive role is why the Oba is often referred to as the traditional ruler and cultural head of all religions in the town. The Oba's attendance at these festivals reassures the community of their dedication to harmony and progress. The town thrives under a peaceful Kingship. Additionally, the Oba often provides directives for these ceremonies to avoid clashes or disruptions and ensures the rightful execution of each festival.

For instance, during the Oro Festival, where women are traditionally prohibited from witnessing certain activities, the Oba's authority is vital. Their blessing and approval prevent conflicts, such as scheduling overlaps or disputes over territorial rights. This festival, which traditionally lasts for seven nights, may sometimes be initiated by the Oba to ward off perceived threats to the town's wellbeing.

HIGHLIGHTS OF AGO-IWOYE'S FESTIVALS

The Empire Day Festival: This festival was a vibrant and colourful celebration, particularly cherished by schoolchildren. Regardless of religious affiliation, pupils from various primary schools would gather at Imososi Wesley School on the selected day. The event was designed to showcase their unity and skills in parade drills while saluting the British flag, symbolising the town's connection to the British Commonwealth. Each school marched in orderly lines, saluting the flag held by a senior town official in the school field. A particularly memorable feature was the beautifully decorated swinging pole carried by the Imososi Primary Wesley School. The pole, accompanied by rhythmic music and skilful swinging, captivated spectators, especially when wielded by a tall and charismatic student known as 'Sophy.' Her performances became legendary during her primary school years. While the Oba's presence was a significant aspect of this ceremony, the Muslim community was often observed without formal representation.

The Agemo Festival: The Agemo Festival drew people from diverse religious backgrounds. It featured two types of Agemos, including the Agemo Eleni, who performed concealed within a mat. Due to the sacred nature of the festival, multi-storey buildings near the performance area had to be evacuated to prevent accidental glimpses of the Agemo. Women and girls formed the majority of the audience, coming to pray for prosperity or suitable marriage partners. While the Oba rarely attended in person, a delegation carrying his staff of office often represented him.

The Oshugbo Festival: Considered one of the earliest inherited festivals, the Oshugbo Festival holds sacred significance. Its rituals are predominantly male-dominated, with activities conducted in a secluded compound inaccessible to women. During anniversaries, the Oshugbo members prepared feasts, often attracting young boys who were eager for a share of the food. Historically, the Oshugbo served as a judicial body, akin to a supreme court, where grave matters, including executions, were deliberated upon. The Oba's involvement in their ceremonies remains confidential, reflecting the sanctity of their practices.

The Olorisa Festival: The Olorisa Festival was led by a single individual, the renowned Hassani Olorisa. His shrine, located in a swampy area, was both revered and feared. On festival days, crowds gathered to witness the captivating dances of Hassani's four wives, whose performances drew visitors from neighbouring towns. Hassani's contributions to traditional culture earned him recognition, including participation in the 1977 African Festival in Lagos. After his passing, the Olorisa tradition dwindled due to a lack of successors.

The Sango Festival: As one of the oldest Yoruba religious practices, the Sango Festival honoured the god of thunder. Before the advent of Christianity and Islam, it was celebrated annually with elaborate rituals and offerings. Strict observances ensured women were informed well in advance to avoid inadvertently witnessing forbidden rites. Though human sacrifices were historically part of such ceremonies, modern practices have evolved. The Oba's stance on the Sango Festival often indicated a preference for newer religious customs.

The Egungun Festival: The Egungun, or masquerade festival, blends spirituality and spectacle. Many attendees view it as a time for prayer and renewal, hoping for prosperity or solutions to personal challenges. Masquerades vary in attire and opulence, with wealthier sponsors showcasing elaborate regalia. Songs, dances, and unique rituals, such as dousing masquerades in water, create an atmosphere of excitement, particularly for children. There was one particular masquerade whose appearance was truly spectacular, known as 'Baba Muda.' The name originated from a devoted Muslim who gave it to his son, thereby becoming popularly identified by it. His devotion to Islam was evident; he named his son by his faith, signifying his adherence to Islamic traditions from birth. Despite his dedication, including performing the five daily prayers and attending Friday Jumu'ah services, he faced challenges. He remained childless for many years, even though he had four wives. His prayers yielded no results. Compelled by conviction, he sought counsel from the Ifa oracle, who advised him to join the masquerade festival. He was assured that this act would transform his circumstances, promising him numerous children. In the first year, he participated in the festival, he paraded through the town with his wives, who surrounded him in a show of support. During the procession, he sang a song to narrate his struggles and explain his decision to embrace the masquerade tradition. The lyrics went: **'Omo logbe mi se o, Omo logbe mi se o a, Imale ki reku omo logbe mi se'**, Which translates roughly to: 'It was the issue of childlessness that compelled me to join the masquerades, even though it is not customary for a Muslim to do so.' Within a year, all his wives became pregnant and delivered safely. He enthusiastically approached the ritual, fully supported by his wives, and their obedience to the Ifa oracle's directives was rewarded. Some masquerades have teams of young men who carry sticks used to strike one another, leaving only light marks playfully. However, they refrain from extending this activity to the spectators, ensuring everyone can enjoy the festivities without sustaining any injuries. When the town faced serious challenges, the Oba would summon the traditional worship leaders to the palace, requesting a week-long ceremony for the benefit of the community. The Ebumawe's request was always honoured, and after the ceremonies, the town often overcame its difficulties. During festivals, masquerades paid homage to the Oba in his palace, showcasing their dancing skills.

The Osugbo Festival: The 'Osugbo' society, another traditional institution, has waned in significance with the advent of Christianity and Islam, which have ridiculed indigenous religions as pagan and satanic. In the 1950s, each quarter in Ago-Iwoye had an 'Iledi', a unique compound for Osugbo members. These buildings featured large halls with cubicles for storing sacred items hidden from the uninitiated. Women were strictly forbidden from entering or even approaching the compound.

The Osugbo hall was a sacred space for elderly men to conduct rituals and make crucial decisions. However, what intrigued the younger generation was the special food prepared during ceremonies–*ebe,* made from yam and ram meat. This exclusive meal was a significant attraction for boys. The decline of Osugbo is attributed to the erosion of its buildings, constructed from mud, as well as a lack of maintenance–a reflection of Africa's broader challenges with preserving cultural heritage.

The Sango Festival: The Sango Festival was once an annual celebration of Yoruba heritage. However, modern perceptions, including the association of indigenous practices with primitivism and satanic rituals, have discouraged younger generations from participating. Sango, a powerful deity, was believed to bless devotees and curse those who disobeyed its commands. The Sango shrine at Ita Ale, central to the town, was respected for its spiritual potency, with stories of mysterious deaths deterring attempts to destroy it.

The Ojude Oba Festival: It is an annual event that brings the community together to honour the Oba. It is an opportunity for the *Egberegbe* (age groups) to celebrate and showcase their contributions. Each group is assigned specific responsibilities, such as organising musicians, drinks, and attire. Recently, the current Ebumawe celebrated his 20th anniversary on the throne at the Wosam Event Centre, where many individuals received chieftaincy titles.

The Isese Festival: It is a celebration of the Yoruba indigenous religion, and has been recognised as a public holiday in many southwestern Nigerian states. However, the federal government has yet to declare it a national holiday, raising questions about equal representation of Nigeria's diverse religious practices.

Nigeria's complexity is evident in its economic, religious, tribal, and political dimensions. Historically, colonial administrators prioritised holidays reflecting their Christian practices, such as Christmas, Boxing Day, and Easter. In contrast, Muslim festivals like Eid al-Kabir, Eid al-Fitr, and Mawlid are also observed but lack the same universal recognition.

The need to respect and preserve all cultural and religious heritages in Nigeria remains a pressing issue for fostering unity and equity among the nation's diverse peoples.

CHAPTER EIGHTEEN
MODERN CHRISTIANITY

In one of the most memorable sermons, I have heard in various churches I've visited or been a member of–reflecting my tendency to seek variety in all aspects of life, including fellowship and social circles–I was reminded of the profound ways in which God tests the faith of His believers. Over the years, I've attended churches of different denominations, including the Catholic Church, the Redeemed Christian Church of God (RCCG), the Christ Gospel Apostolic Church (CGAC), the Christ Apostolic Church (CAC), the Synagogue Church of All Nations, and the Celestial Church of Christ (CCC), particularly during my marriage to a member of the latter.

One recurring theme in these sermons was the idea that God sometimes allows challenges to befall His believers–not as punishment but as a means of testing their faith, spiritual resilience, and trust in Him. These trials are meant to strengthen believers, leading them to a higher spiritual level once they demonstrate faithfulness and perseverance. Running from one challenge to another without anchoring oneself in God's plan often leads to confusion and prolongs the difficulty. Faith and sanctification, therefore, are critical measures of trust in God.

It amazes me when I hear people say, 'I don't want problems', as if life's challenges can always be avoided. In some cases, individuals invite problems through deliberate or unintentional actions, while in others, problems arrive unbidden. As true worshippers of God–be they Christians or Muslims–the only option is to seek divine guidance and solutions rather than relying solely on human effort, which may complicate or prolong the resolution.

Take the example of a bullied child. Parents naturally resist standing idly by when their child is humiliated, as such experiences can harm the child's confidence and hinder their potential for years to come. Many parents have advised their children to defend themselves, even quoting the biblical adage, 'An eye for an eye', despite its contradiction to lawful behaviour. Schools, tasked with addressing bullying, often diffuse situations temporarily, but long-term solutions are elusive. Sadly, reports of children driven to suicide by persistent bullying are a sobering reminder of these failures.

Bullying can stem from superficial differences–such as skin colour, accent, height, or body type–that are beyond one's control. Even dialects, reflecting diverse heritages, have become targets of ridicule. Whether West Indian, African, Asian, Chinese, or American, dialects reflect identity, not inferiority.

I abhor violence in all its forms. A society that respects diversity–like the United Kingdom, known for its multiculturalism–must recognise that race, religion, ethnicity, and culture are not choices but inherent traits. Human dignity must be upheld, and grievances must be addressed constructively.

The principle in human resources management that 'there are

no bad workers, only bad managers' underlines the importance of fair treatment. While employers may reserve the right to dismiss unsuitable employees, workers' rights to fair treatment are equally valid. This tension often leads to tribunal cases, where impartial adjudication is critical.

The government's Social Services Department was established to protect vulnerable members of society, such as women and children, from abuse. However, their interventions can sometimes cause additional trauma. Consider the scenario where a father, after decades of contributing to his family, is removed from his home due to an emergency call from his wife. While such actions are necessary in genuine cases of abuse, they can also fracture families irreparably.

Even more concerning is the rise of children threatening to report their parents for minor disciplinary actions. Cases, where children misuse emergency services to exert control over their parents, highlight the erosion of familial authority. Parents find themselves unable to guide their children effectively, constrained by societal norms and governmental overreach.

The issue extends to broader societal challenges. The prevalence of youth gangs, knife crime, and declining discipline correlates with changes in family dynamics and educational policies. Private schools, often associated with stricter discipline, historically administered corporal punishment, a practice denied in public schools. While controversial, this disparity has arguably contributed to differing behavioural outcomes.

Family breakdowns further exacerbate societal challenges. Stories of betrayal, abandonment, and domestic violence fill the news, often culminating in tragic outcomes. For instance, cases of individuals harming their children or spouses out of jealousy or despair underscore the fragility of modern relationships.

Injustice within the social services system is another pressing issue. Instances where children are removed from young mothers due to presumed incompetence–without allowing them to prove otherwise–are both heart-breaking and potentially damaging. Such actions, though well-intentioned, often lead to long-term trauma. Legal remedies exist but are frequently inaccessible due to financial constraints or systemic biases.

In conclusion, the complexities of modern life require a balance between individual responsibility, family cohesion, and institutional support. While the government and society play essential roles in addressing challenges, empowering families and fostering values of compassion, respect, and discipline remain paramount.

CHAPTER NINETEEN
SPEAKING VOLUMES THROUGH THE EYES

There are many ways in which conversations may occur during a close family gathering. In my mother's family, where she and her five siblings convene for formal or informal meetings, the most intriguing interactions often take place during the formal gatherings. These meetings typically address issues concerning individual family members, and they are usually led by my mother and her two eldest sisters, who are regarded as the family's eyes, ears, and nose.

Living in a polygamous family requires heightened sensitivity, caution, and environmental awareness to safeguard oneself and one's children. A recurring characteristic of our family meetings–whether formal or informal–was the way discussions revolved around domestic or marital issues concerning one of my sisters or us boys, my brother and me. History seemed to repeat itself, as my sisters also married into polygamous Muslim households, where competition among wives was inevitable, often resembling a struggle for the metaphorical gold medal of their husband's attention.

My mother, however, chose a different path in her matrimonial home. She focused on ensuring that her children would grow into individuals of significance later in life. She neither engaged in competition nor harboured envy, blame or regret for past events. Yet, there was something extraordinary about the bond between my mother and my eldest sister, popularly known as 'Alhaja Anifat.' Whenever the five siblings gathered, and a discussion ensued, I noticed a peculiar, silent form of communication between my mother and Alhaja. Regardless of the topic under discussion, my mother would often convey her thoughts to Alhaja without speaking a word. A mere exchange of glances sufficed, and Alhaja's countenance would immediately shift in response. She might nod her head subtly, indicating understanding, or shake it gently from side to side, perhaps suggesting disagreement or deferral.

The relationship between my mother and Alhaja was exceptional, akin to the telepathic connection often attributed to twins. People frequently recount stories of twins who, despite being apart for days, can accurately describe each other's location and attire. I once dismissed such tales as fanciful, but witnessing the silent conversations between my mother and Alhaja in my presence convinced me otherwise. It led me to believe that some individuals are endowed with a unique connection–perhaps akin to twins–despite arriving in the world at different times and through separate channels.

Tragically, Alhaja passed away in a motor accident in Funtua, Northern Nigeria. The suddenness of her death devastated my mother beyond consolation. She became reclusive, rejecting solace and gradually ceasing her usual activities, including her trading and welcoming visitors. Within six months of Alhaja's death, my mother suffered a severe stroke. She lived with the illness for another seven years before passing away. To me, her death was far from peaceful, as the physical and emotional pain she endured remains indelibly etched in my memory. The loss of my two sisters marked the greatest shock of my life. During my time abroad, my elder sister became highly successful in kola nut trading and was honoured with the title of *Iyasuna*–the leader of the Muslim women in our community.

The silent communication between my mother and Alhaja reminded me of a political allegation involving Dr Sanya Dojo Onabamiro and Chief Obafemi Awolowo. Dr Onabamiro accused Chief Awolowo of conducting clandestine sub-meetings during general cabinet sessions through subtle eye contact and gestures with select members. This accusation was seen as divisive, as it implied the creation of a meeting within a meeting. While such allegations might not constitute grounds for a treasonable felony in a democratic dispensation, in the unpredictable landscape of Nigerian politics, anything is possible.

CHAPTER TWENTY

UNCOMMON EXPERIENCES IN AGO-IWOYE

For those born over 55 years ago anywhere in Africa, the experience of rural living is an indelible memory, one that the present generation may never fully understand. People of my age were fortunate to live through, enjoy, and witness the transformation of rural Africa during a period marked by significant changes in lifestyle, living standards, and an environmental revolution.

Some were born and raised in the bustling towns that are now classified as cities, such as Lagos and Ibadan–places that existed long before their arrival. Others, like me, were born during an era often described as 'the dark time', a time when infrastructure was non-existent. We were fortunate to witness the days of no electricity, no tarred roads, and no taxis within towns. When cars passed by on the road, we waved at the occupants in a gesture of admiration, even as they smiled at what could only be described as our poverty and misfortune. We didn't know them, nor could we identify who they were, yet this interaction carried a certain charm.

The town of Ago-Iwoye belonged to this category of settlements until December 1959, the year electricity was introduced. It was a significant moment, likely aimed at preparing the community for the independence celebrations of 1960. Reflecting on the 1940s and 1950s, I recall a lifestyle so rooted in nature that it feels almost surreal compared to the advancements of today. It was a time of transition–from the simplicity of nature to the complexities brought by science, technology, and development.

Some readers, particularly those from my town, may criticise me for recounting these experiences. Others may dismiss or even ridicule my efforts to preserve these memories for those who lacked similar experiences. Yet, as all religious teachings affirm, the truth will prevail, making one whole.

Ago-Iwoye was well known to its neighbours for various reasons, many of which were coloured by myths and tales. Friends from Ijebu-Ode, for instance, often taunted me in social gatherings, recounting hypothetical theories about my town's people. One persistent story claimed that men from Ago-Iwoye disguised themselves as women to solicit payment for immoral acts in Ijebu-Ode. My response was always measured: 'Blessed are those who see one and treat him as a fool, but woe to the person who allows himself to be played as a fool.' This usually silenced further questions.

Another tale questioned whether the people of Ago-Iwoye were so fierce when angered that they fought with cutlasses. My retort was simple: 'Only an idiot would fail to defend himself with whatever means available.' I often invited them to search me for weapons, an offer that typically provoked laughter.

Historically, it was common for towns to ridicule one another.

People of Ijebu-Ode, for example, would refer to neighbours dismissively by extending their left hand. Similarly, the people of Ibadan seldom appreciated the efforts of Ijebus. Such inter-town rivalry has been recorded throughout history.

One infamous chapter was the political turmoil of the Western Region during the *Wet ẹ period*, marked by arson and chaos. People of Ago-Iwoye were implicated, with names like Mojeed Ogberegede becoming legendary. He was reputedly impervious to gunshots and machetes, and his ability to appear and disappear from battlefields was likened to the Prophet Muhammad's hejira. During that era, another figure, a boy nicknamed 'Ajamiroku', gained notoriety for his resilience. Tales of his invincibility included enduring physical trials without harm and causing fires by merely staring at a house.

Ago-Iwoye was also a hub of merriment during festive seasons. Renowned musicians like Hubert Ogunde, Moses Olaiya, and I.K. Dairo often performed there. However, such events sometimes devolved into chaos, sparked by trivial disputes or the actions of unruly locals. In contrast, private celebrations such as naming ceremonies, burials, and chieftaincy installations were well-organised and peaceful, often featuring esteemed musicians like Haruna Ishola and Ligali Mukaiba.

A peculiar practice in Ago-Iwoye during my youth was the kidnapping of young women, often orchestrated by men seeking their hands in marriage. These incidents were rarely reported to the police, even though a station existed nearby. Instead, they were resolved through negotiations led by respected elders. The lack of legal intervention and the cultural acceptance of such acts remain a subject of intrigue and reflection.

Today, memories of Ago-Iwoye evoke both nostalgia and curiosity. Those who have visited often recall the vibrant parties and the hospitality of its people, leaving with a desire to return. These recollections, though deeply personal, form a tapestry of experiences that define the essence of my hometown.

That particular night of the kidnapping, the man in question had to maintain utmost secrecy. He needed to justify why he had decided to abduct that particular woman.

Various reasons were given for his actions, but most were untenable within the legal framework. Kidnapping has always been a serious crime with no valid justification. It deprives the victims' families of their fundamental human rights, instils fear and panic, and leaves them traumatised with the dread that their loved one might be harmed or killed.

The most common excuse was that the man had been in a relationship with the woman for some time. He had spent significant sums of money on her but had recently observed her with another man. Fearing she might leave him for her new lover, he felt compelled to act as he did. However, does such an excuse–potentially imaginative, fabricated, or unfounded–justify the heinous act of kidnapping?

Another reason often cited was that they had been together for a long time, during which he had devoted all his love to her and spent a fortune assisting her family. However, when he asked her to formalise their relationship, she developed cold feet, and he feared she might disappear from his life entirely.

In instances where the man's family supported the act, the next step would involve finding a respected member of the community to act as a mediator between the two families. This individual would serve as the conduit for communication, relaying messages between the man's and the woman's families.

The mediator's primary task was to contact the woman's family to assure them of her safety and well-being. Understandably, the woman's parents and relatives, unaware of her exact location or condition, would react with horror and disbelief. The notion of someone being so callous as to abduct another family's beloved daughter was unfathomable.

Initially, the mediator–often an elderly person with a diplomatic demeanour–would withhold specific details, such as the name of the man's family or the location where the woman was being held. These details would only emerge once the mediator had gained the trust of the woman's family and secured assurances that she was unharmed and being cared for by the man's parents or relatives. The ultimate goal of the mediator's mission was to facilitate a resolution by encouraging the woman's family to outline their terms for a peaceful settlement, ideally culminating in a formalised relationship between the man and the woman.

In most cases I have encountered, such mediation led to peaceful resolutions. However, this was often contingent upon the woman's family or their chosen representative being granted the opportunity to meet with her and seek her opinion on how to proceed.

It is worth noting that, in some instances, members of the man's family might resort to questionable means to influence the woman's feelings. This included administering various concoctions intended to make her develop affection for the man and accept the marriage. Whether these methods were effective remains a matter of speculation, and I leave it to my readers to draw their conclusions or seek insight from their elders on the efficacy of what was colloquially referred to as 'black magic' in those days.

CHAPTER TWENTY- ONE

TALES OF MY HOMETOWN

Permit me to digress briefly to provide more details about what made the people of Ago-Iwoye feared by residents of other towns. During the leadership of Chief Obafemi Awolowo as the Premier of the Western Region of Nigeria, and later as the leader of the Opposition in the Federal Parliament, election campaigns often turned tumultuous. Political opponents employed all manner of tactics, including assassination attempts and disruptions of rallies. It was during this era that Chief Awolowo required the services of a special driver capable of ferrying him to safety under dangerous circumstances.

This daunting responsibility fell to Dauda Odumuyiwa, popularly known as 'Dauda Tinko', a native of Ago-Iwoye. Dauda's unparalleled skill behind the wheel made him legendary. It was widely believed that he could manoeuvre Chief Awolowo's car out of any ambush or hostile crowd with ease, leaving even the fiercest opposition bewildered. His methods, though unscientific, were effective, and he consistently succeeded in keeping the leader safe. When Dauda was at the wheel, his ability to evade danger was near-miraculous.

Ironically, death, that inevitable end, unexpectedly came to him. While driving between Ago-Iwoye and Ibadan, Dauda's car collided with a stationary trailer, leading to his untimely demise. The man many considered invincible and untouchable paid the ultimate price. May his noble and respected soul rest in perfect peace. Amen.

Another significant story that shook the Western Region occurred during the political upheaval between the Action Group of Nigeria (AG) and the Nigerian National Democratic Party (NNDP), led by Chief Samuel Ladoke Akintola. One notable figure in the NNDP, Odunfunlade, a chieftain from Ijebu-Ode, became infamous for his overconfidence and hostility towards political opponents. Backed by the ruling Federal Government, Odunfunlade acted as a conduit for the suppression of opposition figures, often boasting of his ability to humble opponents unchallenged.

Odunfunlade once declared that he would visit Ago-Iwoye to teach the town's political thugs–opponents of his party–a lesson. His reputation instilled fear and his mere mention was enough to send people fleeing. On the appointed day, he entered Ago-Iwoye, unaware that the town had prepared for his arrival. Opposition supporters had set up roadblocks at every entry and exit point, waiting to intercept him.

Rather than turning back when confronted, Odunfunlade attempted to force his way through, injuring several people as he sped into the town. His actions only fuelled the anger of his pursuers, who mobilised in larger numbers to ensure he would not escape unscathed. Realising the gravity of the situation, he initially sought refuge at the compound of Chief Akin

Oshuntoye, a former Action Group stalwart who had defected to the opposition. However, upon noticing he was being followed, Odunfunlade made several futile attempts to escape the town, only to encounter more roadblocks.

Eventually, he returned to Chief Oshuntoye's residence, abandoning his car and seeking shelter inside. Armed with a gun, he began firing at his pursuers, though his shots caused no casualties. His attackers soon discovered that Odunfunlade was heavily fortified with charms, believed to render him impervious to bullets and blades. This assurance had emboldened him, but his adversaries, undeterred, overpowered and neutralised his defences.

In the final moments, Chief Oshuntoye himself had to flee, leaping from a window to avoid being implicated in the chaos. Trapped and outnumbered, Odunfunlade was dragged out, his charms stripped away, and subjected to public humiliation. He was ultimately thrown from an upper-floor window and finished off by the gathered mob. The scene was reminiscent of the Yoruba adage: 'When two elephants fight, the grass suffers most.'

This violent episode served as a grim reminder of the political volatility of the time, leaving behind shattered lives, destroyed property, and a deep sense of loss.

CHAPTER TWENTY-TWO
LIVING IN A GLASS HOUSE

For one reason or another, I have always remembered my educational mentors. Everyone has a reason to admire someone and often aspires to follow in their footsteps. Even individuals engaged in dishonest practices–419 scams, fraudulent *Yahoo* activities, and ritualistic ventures–likely admire someone within their trade who has succeeded without consequences, avoided imprisonment, and displayed a flamboyant lifestyle. Such a person might command attention at social gatherings with their ostentatious display of ill-gotten wealth. Similarly, some individuals admire a particular lifestyle and strive to emulate it, while others idolise womanisers, desiring to be seen with different women on every occasion. However, they forget the adage: 'Things too sweet to the taste end in sour indigestion.' Ultimately, this pursuit is frowned upon by a decent society.

My mentor was an educationist, just a few years my senior. I can confidently state that I knew him from his early teenage years. Ironically, we attended the same primary school, where he was so competent and influential that, after completing his Modern Three teacher training course, he was invited to return as a teacher. He later furthered his education at the Teacher

Training College, popularly known as Ijabcol, in Shagamu. Humbly, he returned to our primary school to continue his teaching career, greatly elevating the teaching profession. His passion inspired many young scholars to pursue careers in education.

At one point, he gained the opportunity to study at the University of Ibadan, where he majored in Economics. While at university, luck favoured his humility, leading to opportunities that may have seemed unfortunate to others but propelled him forward. For instance, he became active in student union activities and was elected Secretary of the Union. During the height of Nigeria's civil war, known as the Biafran War, the Federal Government sought to demonstrate to the international community that the conflict was not an act of genocide against the Igbos but rather an internal disagreement within a united family that made up Nigeria. To garner global support, the government adopted the *Three Rs* policy–Reconciliation, Rehabilitation, and Reconstruction–to promote national unity.

As part of this initiative, university students were sent overseas to present the government's position to their peers and the international community. My mentor was among the delegation selected to travel to the United Kingdom to advocate for the Federal Government's stance.

After graduating, he partnered with a friend whose father owned a paper business. Together, they took over and transformed the industry, providing the elder man with a comfortable retirement. Over time, he diversified his ventures, transitioning from the paper trade into politics. Always a man of prominence and leadership, he was recognised in every gathering. Warm, accommodating, and profoundly generous, he was known for his unwavering commitment to serving his community and offering support to his friends. His religious devotion earned him the revered title of *Aare Muslim* of Ogun State.

The individual I have been describing from the outset of this narrative is none other than Honourable Minister and Senator Alhaji Jubril Martins Kuye, who once served as Minister of Finance and later as Minister of Industry during Goodluck Jonathan's administration. As I mentioned earlier, he was, and remains, my mentor even after his passing.

In 1959, he taught at Moslem Primary School, Imere, in my hometown, where I was one of his pupils. There was another teacher of the same age, who shared similar characteristics and humour, but Alhaji Kuye's exceptional charisma set him apart. Whether in the classroom, on the sports field, or during social events, he effortlessly blended with his students, making it difficult to distinguish between him and us. His humour and unique personality left an indelible impression, creating cherished memories that I continue to treasure. What a special gift of charisma he possessed!

What impresses me most about him are the proverbs, quotations, and sayings he often referenced during his teaching. One of the presenters on *Journalist Hangout*, Citizen John Usein, frequently quotes past American Presidents during his programme, and this often reminds me of my mentor. Some of these quotations have left an indelible mark on my life's journey to date. Let me recount just a few of them.

The first and most significant was, 'That something is impossible can only be found in the dictionary of fools.' When I went home on the day he shared this in class, the words resonated in my mind for months. They became the foundation for my life's ambitions and transformed the way I viewed the world. This quotation has served as both a bedrock and a constant alarm bell in my life.

In practising politics, my mentor embodied integrity; he said only what he could do and consistently delivered on his promises. He stood apart from the majority of Nigerian politicians, who often speak recklessly, driven by selfish interests. Democracy in Nigeria has turned many politicians into figurative 'birds in the sky', oblivious to the fact that those on the ground are watching them closely and can see the holes in their garments. Such politicians readily make grandiose promises, boasting about achieving the impossible. Their desperation for power often leads them to break the mandates given by the people and discard their campaign manifestos once they achieve their selfish goals.

Nigeria is no longer the country I remember growing up in. A particular video clip I saw on social media shocked me regarding the trajectory of the new generation of politicians and society in general. In the clip, a father called his son, who was living abroad, to remind him of his promise to build a modern family home in their hometown. The father also mentioned that the son's friend, who had travelled abroad at the same time, had already completed a house for his own family and even bought a car for his mother. He urged his son to seek advice from his friend on how he managed to fulfil these obligations.

The son explained that he had visited his friend the previous night, where the friend revealed the secret to his success. However, the revelation was horrifying. The son asked his father if he was aware that the friend's father had died late the previous year, to which the father responded that he knew and had even attended the burial. The son then revealed that his friend had taken him to a herbalist who provided 'medicine' that supposedly enabled his friend to accumulate wealth. The friend had agreed to a ritual sacrifice, which involved using his father's private parts and head. Shockingly, the son confessed that he too had agreed to a similar arrangement, consenting for the herbalist to use his father in the same way, in exchange for wealth.

At this point, the father abruptly ended the call and refused to answer any further calls from his son. The lesson this video imparts is profound. Initially, the father was pressuring his son to achieve wealth by any means, but when he realised he was to be the sacrificial lamb, he immediately disengaged. This story highlights a disturbing reality: some parents push their children towards dangerous and immoral paths in their pursuit of a better life, only to recoil when faced with the personal cost of such actions. The father's reaction serves as a stark reminder of the consequences of misguided ambitions and misplaced priorities.

CHAPTER TWENTY-THREE

THE LIFE OF AJAMIROKU

Ajamiroku was born in the Isamuro quarters of Ago-Iwoye. His parents could not afford to send him for further studies after completing primary six, so he joined notorious groups involved in fighting or defending a political party during the 'Wet e' episode. Being accustomed to taking various drugs and relying on charms to protect himself from being killed, he was lured into testing new charms prepared by herbalists to shield their members from attacks by the opposition party. When the riots eventually came to an end, no one heard from him again. There were only rumours suggesting that he had suffered from mental deterioration or had become disabled, until it was later confirmed that he had passed away under terrible circumstances. May his soul rest in peace.

    The issue surrounding the young boy mentioned in this chapter was deeply tragic and requires examination from a different perspective, particularly regarding the influence of parents on their children. The first area that must be investigated thoroughly is why a young boy of six or seven would decide, or be persuaded, to associate with a dangerous gang. Equally concerning is the involvement of older individuals, who should have been father figures, exploiting him as a guinea pig or treating him as a disposable being for testing various black medicines.

Was it due to undiagnosed mental health challenges, or was he coerced by the financial inducements of people old enough to be his grandfather? Considering his likely background of extreme poverty, he might have struggled to envision a bright future for himself. Crucially, there appears to have been no effort to determine whether he was suffering from any neurological or psychological issues. However, it is beyond doubt that local substances, such as marijuana–commonly referred to as *Apetesi* at the time–and the intoxicating brew *Ogogoro*, widely available at bus garages, may have significantly influenced his circumstances. The pervasive use of marijuana by drivers and their conductors cannot be dismissed as a contributing factor.

Tragically, there seems to have been no attempt to trace the boy's biological background–his uncles, siblings, or extended family–to shed light on his upbringing, behaviour, and social circle, both during and after school hours. This omission is striking given the severity of the case. It is indisputable that inducing or coercing a child of his age into a criminal gang for dangerous activities constitutes a grave criminal offence. Many of the political thugs who exploited the boy had their children and grandchildren safely protected at home.

If there was any truth to the rumour, the boy was reportedly tied by his hands and legs, placed in a mortar, and pounded like yam to test the potency of newly introduced black medicines. These were then distributed among thugs for use in their brutal campaigns to harm or incapacitate political opponents. The goal was to ensure their fighters remained invincible and unaffected by adversaries' black magic.

Sadly, a few months after the political unrest subsided and governance changed in the region, the boy reportedly died. The exact circumstances of his death–whether from illness or other causes–remain unknown. As a result, no lessons could be drawn from the tragedy, and no scientific investigations were conducted. Only God knows how many young boys and men were subjected to such horrific trials and had their lives prematurely cut short in the pursuit of political power. Borrowing from the title of Wole Soyinka's novel, *The Man Died*, this boy's death could similarly be referred to as *And the Boy Died*.

The case of the boy known as *Ajamiroku* demands investigation. Those responsible for drawing him into the gang must be held accountable. Even if some perpetrators have died, their names should be documented in historical records to acknowledge the atrocities committed during their lifetimes. If necessary, Ajamiroku's body could be exhumed and examined scientifically, with any findings used as a study case.

For context, in the United Kingdom, two soldiers who died in 1944 during the Second World War at the ages of 21 and 27 were recently given full military burials with all honours. Their surviving relatives were invited to the ceremonies. When will Africa–and Nigeria in particular–begin to properly honour the sacrifices and struggles of its people, beyond simply commemorating well-known politicians?

CHAPTER TWENTY-FOUR

MUSHAFAU: THE DISABLED BICYCLE REPAIRER AND RENTAL

From my childhood, I have been deeply impressed whenever I encountered someone with a visible disability who was determined to live a productive life. On the other hand, when I see individuals with disabilities who have resorted to begging, I often feel a profound sense of pity and extend my sympathy to them, provided their state of incapacity is not self-inflicted. The streets, markets, motor parks, and virtually every vacant space–under bridges and at social event centres–are flooded with beggars. When you take the time to observe this group of people, you may be compelled, albeit without scientific evidence, to conclude that some could redirect their lives towards a more meaningful purpose.

For instance, a person rendered mentally incapacitated by substance abuse, someone severely injured in violent altercations over money at a motor park, or an individual who became an amputee following acts of robbery, whether day or night, might not readily elicit sympathy.

The story of Mushafau, however, is both remarkable and poignant, deserving of admiration for his courage and unwavering determination to provide for himself. His resilience, though understated in the 1950s when urban life was not widely understood, was truly heroic and deserving of a national award. Mushafau's case, as told by those who knew him and his family, was one of unimaginable hardship and sympathy.

According to family accounts, Mushafau's parents had previously lost three children, all of whom had passed away before reaching the age of three. At the time, there were no medical centres available where pregnant women could receive pre-natal or post-natal care. There was no opportunity for unborn children to be medically examined, and childbirth typically occurred under the supervision of local herbalists or community elders rather than qualified doctors and nurses.

Childbirth practices of that era were crude and perilous. The herbalist, with no knowledge of modern prenatal or postnatal testing, might prepare herbal concoctions for a pregnant woman, though there was no scientific evidence to support their efficacy. The prevailing method of childbirth was equally alarming. The husband would be instructed to light a wood fire, and the labouring woman was made to sit as close as possible to the heat, with her back towards the flames. The belief was that the heat would discomfort the baby in the womb, prompting it to 'push itself out.' This primitive practice posed significant risks, often causing deformities or injuries to the child during delivery.

Mushafau's situation was tragic and could be classified as man-made. Family records revealed that his mother had given birth to three other children before him. Each of these children, as if under a malevolent curse, survived to ages three to five but eventually succumbed to mysterious deaths.

The accounts of Mushafau's demise were no less distressing. It was said that, after finishing his dinner one evening, Mushafau approached his mother and calmly informed her that he was about to die. Stricken with panic, having experienced similar scenarios with her other children, she immediately sent for her husband, who had gone to visit a friend. By the time the husband and his companion rushed back, Mushafau had already passed away. They found his lifeless body on the floor and the plate from which he had eaten just minutes earlier still in its place.

The incident irritated the father's friend, and out of anger, he lost control of his emotions. In his fury, he lifted the boy and, noticing he was lifeless, twisted his right leg violently, admonishing him never to return to the family again, declaring, 'Enough is enough. You have caused enough problems and heartbreak for your mother and father.'

It was later reported that the friend's wife became pregnant a few months after this incident and gave birth to a baby boy with a right leg so twisted it could not be straightened to its normal form. Strangely, it was said the boy returned to the man who had twisted his leg, bearing the same deformity, but this time as the man's offspring in a subsequent life. At the boy's birth, some relatives and friends suggested the family should abandon him, claiming he would not survive for long. However, his mother, a strong-willed and devout woman, stood her ground, affirming her faith in God's will and her determination to nurture the child for as long as he lived.

Mushafau, as the boy was named, grew up amid envy from family members and neighbours. Despite having only one functional leg and relying on a wooden pole to support and propel his twisted limb, he was remarkably active in games. At a time when it was astonishing to see such resilience, Mushafau excelled at errands and sports, including running, playing ball games, and hunting birds with a catapult. At primary school, he became a shining star and a source of inspiration, admired by both teachers and his headmaster. He was brilliant, quick to answer questions, displayed excellent handwriting, and rarely lagged in any subject.

Yet, despite his abilities, he could not advance his education beyond the primary school level due to financial constraints. The free education programme introduced by Chief Obafemi Awolowo extended only to primary six, and his parents lacked the resources to send him to secondary school, modern school, or teacher training college. Nonetheless, Mushafau graduated with outstanding results.

Determined to carve a path for himself, Mushafau defied societal expectations that would have relegated him to a life of begging or humiliation. Instead, he apprenticed as a bicycle repairman, despite being unable to ride a bicycle himself. He had a plan: once he set up his own business, his future apprentices could test the bicycles he repaired. During his apprenticeship, he focused on tasks such as patching and reattaching rubber tyres, jobs he could accomplish seated. His ambition and foresight were impressive; he aimed to hire assistants to handle aspects of the trade his physical disability restricted him from performing.

Before completing the mandated three-year apprenticeship, Mushafau's skill and work ethic gained the attention of the community. People frequently brought their bicycles for repairs, often out of curiosity to see the one-legged boy at work. Many even preferred having repairs done at his home, citing reduced rates and overnight service.

When Mushafau eventually gained his freedom, he rented the frontage of a house owned by a respected Alfa in Idode, using the space for his bicycle repair business. The location also served as a bicycle rental centre for young boys from neighbouring areas such as Idode, Okebute, and Ota in Ago-Iwoye. To this day, I would posthumously name the workshop 'Mushafau Bicycle Enterprise.'

In our childhood, we enjoyed patronising his bicycle rental service, paying just one penny (1p) for a 30-minute ride. However, our youthful mischief often led us to return the bicycles late. To avoid confrontation, we would abandon the bicycles at the roadside, shouting to him, 'Mushafau, we've returned your bicycle! Come and get it!' Naturally, this provoked his anger, but he tolerated our antics because we were regular customers who helped sustain his livelihood.

Sadly, I have not seen Mushafau since 1960 and know nothing of his whereabouts. I recall his family home near Okodo, next to the site called 'Atenda', where my father partnered with Mago in a cattle-slaughtering business. Mushafau also shared a family connection with the late Ogunnusi, nicknamed *Kadikadi* by my brother Oseni, who was a musician with the late Tunde Nightingale.

The story of Ago-Iwoye, as I experienced it in the 1940s, 1950s, and 1960s, would be incomplete without recognising individuals like Mushafau. Their lives stand in stark contrast to the normalised culture of begging that was prevalent at the time. Mushafau's determination and industrious spirit made him a role model, proving that history should not be dominated solely by political figures, chieftains, or the controversial but also by the unsung heroes who inspired future generations.

CHAPTER TWENTY-FIVE
IWOYE TOWN CENTRE

METHODIST CHURCH, ITA

The only recognised centre in Ago-Iwoye was a place called 'Ita Ale'. It was a popular gathering spot for traders, who brought their products for sale at night, seven days a week. The site was an open space, except for those fortunate enough to have houses around it, who created frontage shops and used any available extra space to allow traders to set up temporary kiosks. These kiosks were erected only in the evenings and dismantled after the nightly trade. Ita Ale offered a wide variety of goods, and there was no commodity or produce you couldn't find there between 7:00 and 11:00pm.

It was a delight to wander through the market, especially when all the traders had settled behind their wares. Goods were either displayed in portable containers or neatly spread out on moderately sized flat tables made of wood. Traders arranged their products in ways that would attract the attention of passersby, enticing potential buyers to purchase and take their chosen items home.

Every trader was required to bring their kerosene-filled lamps to the night market. These lamps were typically made of steel with a top handle and were considered a modern means of lighting the environment. Alternatively, traders could use the traditional *atupa*, a lamp fashioned with a wool thread that soaked kerosene to sustain its flame. These lamps, crafted by blacksmiths known locally as 'Agbedes', often included a mechanism to adjust the brightness. The spectacle of Ita Ale bathed in the varied light of these lamps made the market appear like a scattering of moons in the evening sky.

There was an impressive range of products available at the night market: kerosene, clothing materials, fresh meat, cow legs, dried fish, fresh fish, yams in various sizes and prices, and eggs–both fresh and boiled–from local bush fowls. The eggs, smaller in size but sweeter in taste than those from farm-raised poultry, were a particular treat. The market also provided a social hub, where visitors moved between rows of goods, viewing prices, making jokes, and enjoying the vibrant atmosphere.

Many traders transitioned from the day market, held every five days, to the nightly market in hopes of selling more products. Youngsters like myself took advantage of the market's lively atmosphere. After hawking *moin-moin* (bean pudding) during the day, I would bring any leftovers to Ita Ale in the evening. It was a chance for us to indulge in playful activities, such as buying boiled eggs and engaging in a game where we knocked one egg against another to see which remained intact.

The absence of electricity in the town at that time added to the charm of the market, as every trader brought their light to illuminate their wares. The market spanned from 'Ita Kekere' (meaning 'Small market') to a place called Idi Konga (the government well), and it opened every evening for business.

Ita Ale held significance beyond commerce. It was recognised as the town's centre and played an important role in its spiritual history. It was the birthplace of African traditional religion, including the worship of Songo, the Yoruba god of thunder. The 'Ile Songo', previously mentioned in earlier chapters, was a modest structure, approximately 6 by 6 feet, built centuries ago from mud. Remarkably, this small house had withstood the test of time, enduring annual heavy rains, erosions, and floods without collapsing. There seemed to be an inexplicable, perhaps supernatural, power that kept the structure intact through the centuries.

The only person I recall remaining devoted to the Songo deity was a woman known as *Orisha jugbe*, meaning 'You cannot carry or remove the Songo from its established place.'

The Muslim community also made their mark in the town, acquiring land near Ita Ale to establish Ako Moslem Primary School and their Central Mosque, where Friday Jumat prayers were held. Interestingly, the Central Mosque was just two feet away from the Ile Songo. Despite sharing such close quarters for over half a century, tensions arose when some modern Muslim devotees viewed the presence of the Songo shrine as an affront. Attempts to demolish the structure, however, were met with mysterious deaths among those involved, putting an end to further destruction.

Christian missionaries also left their footprint near Ita Ale. The first Methodist Church, linked to the Wesleyan tradition, was established nearby, following their European preference for spacious, fenced properties. They secured land a short distance from the town centre–just a two-minute walk–and also built the first Wesley Primary School at the beginning of Ishamuro Road. This choice reflected the Christian community's appreciation for large, open spaces where their institutions could flourish.

The fourth religious body that played a role in the use of the Ita-Ale was the Alagemos, adherents of the traditional religion practised in the Ishamuro quarter. Their anniversary ceremony occurred on a single day each year and also took place at Ita-Ale. Not far from the Moslem Primary School Ita-Ale, there was a small bush, which served as the base for the various groups of devotees and participants from across Yorubaland who gathered to grace the occasion.

On the day of the ceremony, representatives of the Agemo from different towns would assemble in this bush and at a nearby dumping ground specifically designated for their purposes during the celebrations. It was here that they began their rituals, performing sacrifices as a precursor to their ceremonial outing later in the evening. The Agemos always passed by the side of the Ako Moslem Primary School and the Central Mosque before emerging into the open space where the main ceremony was conducted.

Women and children made up the largest segment of the audience at the finale of the anniversary celebration. One of the most remarkable aspects of the event was the fervent manner in which the women prayed–for themselves, their husbands, their children, and their wider family. They sought blessings from the god of Agemo with unwavering passion and energy. However, given that many of these women came from polygamous households, it was evident that their prayers rarely extended to include their husbands' other wives. It was clear they refrained from cursing the women who divided their husband's attention, but nor did they pray for them. It was obvious that no woman prayed to become a second wife, nor did any wish for their husband to take another wife after her.

CHAPTER TWENTY-SIX

THE CAUSES OF TEENAGE RITUALISM

Nigeria has become a nation where actions once deemed forbidden or ungodly during my youth are now regarded as socially acceptable. In the 1940s, 1950s, and early 1960s, it was considered taboo for one person to cause the death of another outside the jurisdiction of law enforcement. Such actions were unthinkable and morally reprehensible. I refer to this period as the *Old Testament*. However, the *New Testament* of societal behaviour has unfolded, introducing new chapters and paradigms, particularly among the youth.

During my formative years, we were taught that human life was sacred and that we must avoid any situation that could lead to the loss of life. This value was deeply rooted in the teachings of both the Holy Bible and the Holy Quran, which served as moral compasses in our upbringing, both at home and in school, including Arabic lessons. We were instilled with the understanding that since we cannot create life, we have no right to take it, either intentionally or through negligence. This ethos fostered a sense of community and responsibility. If we perceived any danger that could harm another's life or health, we would promptly warn others, ensuring that the entire community was protected from potential calamities.

The *New Testament*, as I term it, reflects a reverse in these values. It is evident in the actions of the younger generation, who, driven by greed, intentionally or negligently endanger others' lives. This moral decline has manifested starkly in Nigeria's political sphere. A pervasive lust for power and wealth has overridden principles of morality, fair play, and godliness. Politicians now resort to despicable acts to undermine opponents, forgetting the fundamental nature of politics as a contest where one wins and another loses, with the pendulum potentially swinging in subsequent elections.

The methods employed include consultations with religious and spiritual leaders, including pastors, Malams, herbalists, and others, to seek powers that can destabilise opposing political camps. Thuggery, violence, and vote-buying are well-documented in our political history. These acts are no longer exaggerations but grim realities:

1. Distribution of cash gifts to voters.
2. Provision of five yards of fabric or five-kilo bags of rice as bribes.
3. Snatching of ballot boxes.
4. Manipulation of vote counts.
5. Announcing results before vote counting is completed.
6. Fabricating election results outright.

To ensure compliance, some are subjected to sinister rituals, such as shedding blood or stepping over weapons to instil fear.

Bribery of electoral officials, even those of high standing like professors, further corrupts the democratic process. A case in point involved a regional electoral commissioner (REC), a respected professor, who announced incomplete results. This breach of trust has caused the public to lose faith in such appointees, irrespective of their academic or social standing.

Ballot box snatching, a tactic used to disrupt vote counting or transportation, underscores the desperation of politicians. Alarmingly, these perpetrators are often recognised figures within their communities, where they are meant to serve as role models.

This degeneration is not confined to politics. It has seeped into broader society, influencing teenagers and youths to adopt these sinister behaviours. Social events highlight another disturbing trend. For example, musicians contracted for events may prioritise guests capable of extravagant money spraying–a grotesque display of wealth uninvestigated by authorities. These individuals are often accompanied by uniformed police officers, who, rather than serving the public, act as escorts, clearing pathways for the ostentatiously wealthy.

It is inconceivable that the Inspector General of Police would approve such misuse of personnel. Yet, in today's Nigeria, even criminals and questionable characters have access to police escorts, a privilege that symbolises the depths of societal decay.

WHY AND WHEN DID WE BECOME SO BRUTAL AND INHUMAN TO EACH OTHER?

This display of ill-gotten wealth, for which its source cannot be presented to the Audit Office or the public, has become a troubling norm. These individuals, whether through registered or unregistered businesses–some purportedly tied to the National Drug Law Enforcement Agency (NDLEA) or illicit bank accounts under the guise of the Central Bank of Nigeria (CBN)–freely flaunt their riches. They throw bundles of naira notes at the feet of musicians with impunity, acting as though they are above the law. These musicians, in turn, sing their praises, elevating their benefactors beyond their true worth. Meanwhile, the audience–dancing, clapping, and laughing–resembles a scene of forced joy akin to Jewish detainees at Nazi concentration camps.

The reckless spraying of money at social gatherings serves as a platform for teenagers and youths in this country to emulate these behaviours. This ambition to surpass the social and financial status of their predecessors has driven many down perilous paths. On several occasions, when passing by student hostels in Ago-Iwoye, I have marvelled at the sophisticated and exorbitantly priced cars parked within and outside these residences. It's baffling to witness students, supposedly in the throes of learning, possessing and maintaining such luxury vehicles. What cars, one wonders, would these individuals aspire to own once they enter the workforce–assuming they secure employment in the current economic climate?

Many of these students come from modest backgrounds, rendering their ostentatious lifestyles inexplicable. Among the cars owned by students in 2023 were high-end brands such as Range Rover Sports, Discovery, Evoque, Toyota Cruisers, Highlanders, Venzas, Volvo SUVs, and other exotic makes. This unchecked ambition often leads them to unethical and forbidden memberships in secret societies. The allure of wealth drives some to embrace notoriety as 'Yahoo boys' or scammers, emptying bank accounts of unsuspecting victims while taking perverse pride in their 'success.' The victims, left financially and emotionally devastated, often consider suicide, even as the perpetrators laugh at their exploits.

What is even more troubling is the gap between the students and their lecturers. Professors, earning modest salaries and tasked with providing for their families, often cannot afford such luxuries, even with car loans. This disparity breeds disrespect. Students, emboldened by their ill-gotten wealth or cult affiliations, intimidate lecturers to pass them in the examinations they refuse to study for, resorting to bribery or threats of violence to achieve their ends.

Recently, a more horrifying trend has emerged: ritual killings for monetary gain. Some students believe that by harvesting body parts for ritualistic purposes, as instructed by herbalists, they can achieve instant riches without detection or consequence. These acts, promising wealth within a month, leave their perpetrators unrepentant and dismissive of potential moral or psychological repercussions.

Equally troubling is the desperation among young pastors. Many crave the title of General Overseer (GO) and the financial gains associated with leading large congregations. Some resort to heinous acts under the guise of spiritual activities to attract wealthier church members capable of hefty donations. There are chilling accounts of pastors luring women into false prayer sessions, only to murder them and use their body parts as rituals for the expansion of their churches. These gruesome practices have nothing to do with promoting Christianity; rather, they are driven by a fierce competition for dominance among denominations.

For example, on 23 September 2024, *The Punch* newspaper reported the arrest of a 23-year-old philosophy student, Ayomide Adeleye, from Olabisi Onabanjo University (OOU). He was accused of murdering an 18-year-old church member, Christiana Idowu, who had visited his home under the pretext of repairing her phone. Christiana, an Industrial Training student at Yaba College of Technology, was strangled during the visit. Adeleye then contacted Christiana's mother, demanding a ransom of ₦3million. Although he managed to collect ₦360,000, his attempt to extort further money led to his arrest after law enforcement traced his identity through a SportyBet account linked to his national identity number.

Adeleye's crime highlights the destructive effects of misguided ambitions. Emulating the wealthier students around him, he brutally extinguished the life of an innocent young lady. His story underscores the growing moral decay in a society where the pursuit of wealth eclipses basic humanity.

Human rituals, a universal feature of societies, include rites of worship, oaths, dedications, and ceremonies. While these practices may serve positive purposes elsewhere, in Africa, they are often misused and shrouded in secrecy. Herbalists encouraging individuals to murder loved ones for wealth illustrate a societal greed that disregards the sanctity of life. Those who commit such atrocities forget that they will one day answer for their deeds before a higher power.

We must ask ourselves: why and when did we become so brutal and inhuman to one another?

CHAPTER TWENTY-SEVEN
AGO-IWOYE: A LEGACY OF AGRICULTURE, TRADE, AND CULTURAL HERITAGE

Ago-Iwoye people are renowned and celebrated for their dedication to farming, producing significant agricultural outputs surpassing those of many towns across the country. What set them apart was their dual reputation as industrious farmers and reputable traders. This dual identity compelled each family, within every quarter of the town, to remain rooted in their ancestral villages to focus effectively on farming. Imagine a scenario where a farmer wakes up in his home in a town and travels on foot for five to six hours to his distant farm, only to return the same day to rest and attend to family matters, all while contemplating repeating the journey the next day. How long, one wonders, could such a cycle continue before exhaustion renders the farmer incapable of sustaining such efforts?

The challenges of leaving a farm unattended for weeks or months are equally significant. Uncontrolled weeds quickly overrun recently planted crops, destroying their potential to grow and mature, ultimately preventing the expected harvest. Additionally, the narrow paths leading to farms require consistent use to prevent them from becoming overgrown with fresh grass and thorns, rendering them impassable.

At a time when public transportation was unavailable between Ago-Iwoye and its surrounding village settlements, the people displayed remarkable ingenuity. They built villages comprising mud houses and huts roofed with palm fronds to shelter their families from unpredictable weather. Doors and windows crafted from palm kernel trees provided privacy.

Communal vigilance was an intrinsic part of village life. Any unfamiliar noise could lead to a shouted inquiry of 'Who is there?' If the response was not from a familiar voice, the alarm would be raised, prompting a collective search of every nook and corner to ensure no intruder was hiding.

While farmers laboured in their fields from morning until evening, their wives initially remained in the huts awaiting their return. Over time, however, women began engaging in economic activities, such as trading in town markets or mini-markets in larger villages. They sold essential foodstuffs like salt, sugar, rice, beans, fresh meat, and gari, sustaining their families from day to day. Women also organised themselves, both individually and in teams, to process crops such as cassava into gari, palm kernels into palm oil, and cocoa pods into black soap. These products were carried on their heads to nearby village markets or, in cases of larger production, transported to the main town market, which operated every five days regardless of the day of the week.

In those times, polygamy was seen as a symbol of status and pride. At ceremonies, a man with only one wife might appear ridiculous amongst his peers, who flaunted their two to four wives. This practice, particularly prevalent among tradesmen and public transport drivers, underscored their societal standing.

TRADING AND THE DECLINE OF THE AGO-IWOYE CENTRAL MARKET

Men, too, were pivotal to the town's trading economy, acting as intermediaries between buyers and sellers of commodities like rams, goats, and kola nuts. Some traders faithfully attended every market day, arriving either the night before or early on the day itself. Middlemen earned their compensation from sellers, receiving a percentage of the proceeds for facilitating sales and negotiating favourable prices.

The Ago-Iwoye central market, once a vibrant hub situated along Imere Road at Igan, holds fond memories for many. However, during a recent visit, I observed with profound sadness the dilapidation of this once-thriving centre of commerce. The kola nut section, once bustling with activity, is now abandoned, overtaken by bushes. This stark reality evokes painful memories of the vibrant community of traders from the 1940s to the 1960s, including Hausa traders who packaged kola nuts for distribution across the northern regions.

The stalls, once teeming with goat and sheep sellers, have also become deserted, with only a handful of animals tethered to poles. This area, previously bustling with negotiations and activity, is now a shadow of its former self. Similarly, the abattoir at Oke-Odo, where my father collaborated with Pa Mago to distribute cow parts, now stands unused and derelict.

The fresh meat market, once a hive of activity, is eerily silent, and the site where I once sold *moin-moin* in traditional calabashes is desolate. Today, meat and fish sellers are relegated to the market's entrance, sheltering under umbrellas. I was disheartened to learn that most traders now travel to Ijebu-Igbo to purchase these goods.

PRESERVING OUR HERITAGE

My reflections on this visit reveal a troubling trend: the people of Ago-Iwoye increasingly patronise roadside shops rather than the central market, contributing to its decline. It may be time for the Ebumawe, Otunbas, and traditional elders to explore cultural and spiritual solutions to revive the market's historical status.

As a people blessed with a cultural and spiritual heritage akin to the Israelites and Arabs, it is disheartening that we neglect our ancestral wisdom. While modern malls and elaborately decorated shops may dominate today's shopping landscape, we must safeguard our traditional market systems for future generations.

We cannot allow the heritage we inherited to perish during our time.

CHAPTER TWENTY-EIGHT

THE HISTORY OF NAMING AGE GROUPS (EGBEREGBE)

One of the distinct traditions peculiar to the people of Ago-Iwoye is their ability to identify the group to which they belong through their age. This enables every individual, whether male or female, to determine their place in the community and the name of their age group. The Ebumawe, as the Oba of the town, holds the prerogative and exclusive power to name individuals born within three years, allowing them to associate and identify themselves as belonging to that age group. This tradition has been practised as far back as the history of the town can record.

As mentioned in earlier chapters and pages of this book, the naming of age groups serves several purposes. In the past, the elderly inhabitants of the town were predominantly farmers who lived in villages to facilitate their farming activities. However, they were required to visit the town periodically for various reasons: to oversee the condition of their family homes, ensure their properties were not stolen, participate in annual events such as

Christmas, New Year, and Muslim festivals, and attend celebrations such as birthdays, burials, housewarmings, and other social gatherings involving friends, family members, and associates.

Most importantly, individuals needed to come to town once a month to attend their age group's monthly meeting. These meetings provided an opportunity for people born within a three-year gap to register as members and participate in developmental programmes assigned to their age group by the Ebumawe-in-Council. Such programmes were designed to address matters requiring community attention in the town. Age groups also participated collectively in general social events, including the 'Ojude Oba' festival, the coronation of a new Oba, the installation of new Otunbas, annual coronation festivals, and religious celebrations like Christmas, New Year, Eid-ul-Fitr, and Eid-ul-Adha.

The monthly meetings of the age groups, known as 'Egberegbe' in Ijebu culture, were established decades before the advent of modern European civilisation in Africa. The primary purpose was to enable members of the same age group to identify one another and convene at an agreed location to discuss issues relevant to their group or assignments delegated by the Ebumawe-in-Council. Before the construction of tarred roads in Ago-Iwoye, Egberegbe members were tasked with clearing bushes and grasses along the roadsides. Each age group within a quarter would subdivide itself, allocate portions of the road to smaller groups, and agree on a date for the task.

Any member who failed to participate on the scheduled day faced serious disciplinary measures, including public humiliation. It was customary for the entire age group of the quarter to assemble in front of the defaulter's home, shouting abuses in protest, thereby drawing the attention of neighbours to the offender's actions. In extreme cases, the group was permitted to seize a goat belonging to the offender or someone related to them. The seized goat would be sold, and the proceeds deposited into the group's account. The offender was then obligated to compensate the goat's owner, serving as both punishment and deterrence.

Records in the archives indicate that the naming of age groups is announced by the Ebumawe after thorough consultations with the heads of the quarters.

NAMES AND YEARS OF BIRTH OF AGE GROUPS IN AKILE IJEBU:

1. Basanle (1777)
2. Lowuni (1781)
3. Legbeta (1785)
4. Ile Segun (1787)
5. Motukoya (1793)
6. Moteju (1797)
7. Ile Sanya (1801)
8. Ile Sewo (1805)
9. Ile Ikanigbo (1809)
10. Modaragun (1813)
11. Botewa (1817)
12. Kotetan (1821)
13. Otekase (1825)
14. Kele (1829)
15. Mayegun (1833)
16. Otetumo (1837)

17. Bobado (1841)
18. Mafowoku (1845)
19. Bobaloju (1849)
20. Bobasete (1853)
21. Gbobaniyi (1857)
22. Oriyonote (1861)
23. Majobate (1865)
24. Bobasanya (1869)
25. Arobayo (1873)
26. Obagbuyi (1877)
27. Obaneye (1881)
28. Obayori (1885)
29. Obase (1889)
30. Obabeke (1893)
31. Obalolaiye (1897)
32. Obafowora (1901)
33. Obagoroye (1905)
34. Obangbade (1909)
35. Bobadega (1913)
36. Fibiwoga (1915)
37. Obalolola (1917-1920)
38. Obalolade (1920-1923)
39. Obabosipo (1923-1925)
40. Bobagunwa (1926-1928)
41. Bobasegun (1929-1931)
42. Mafowoku (1932-1935)
43. Olugbadebo (1935-1937)
44. Bobayo (1938-1940)
45. Bobagbuyi (1941-1943)

46. Obaleke (1944-1946)
47. Bobajolu (1947-1949)
48. Obafuwaji (1950-1952)
49. Bobagbimo (1953-1955)
50. Bobakoya (1956-1958)
51. Bobagunte (1959-1961)
52. Gbobaniyi (1962-1964)
53. Jagunmolu (1965-1967)
54. Arobayo (1968-1970)
55. Tobalase (1971-1973)
56. Bobamaiyegun (1974-1976)
57. Obayomi (1977-1979)
58. Bobagunwa (1980-1982)
59. Obaneye (1983-1985)

The naming of the Egberegbe groups applied to the entirety of Ijebu-land, ensuring uniformity across towns. This suggests that the names originated from the reigning Oba of Ijebu-Ode, the capital of Ijebu-land. The names were then disseminated to the Obas and Bales of each town, who announced them to their subjects during appropriate ceremonies. This practice reinforced the authenticity and universality of the age group names and their significance in the cultural identity and governance of Ijebu-land.

OTHER BOOKS BY THE AUTHOR

The Demise of Nigeria Airways Limited

My Experience of Police Detentions in Nigeria and the United Kingdom

Uses of Date of Birth

ABOUT THE AUTHOR

OLATUNJI OLUSANYA is an octogenarian whose passion for writing explores life's complexities and the pressing issues within society. A fervent advocate for justice, human dignity, and societal reform, he draws on decades of experience to offer a deeply personal and insightful perspective on governance, human rights, and social equity.

Born in Ago-Iwoye, Ogun State, Nigeria, Olatunji is deeply rooted in family values and cultural heritage while embracing the importance of adapting to change. His writings aim to illuminate vital social issues, provoke reflection, and inspire action for a fairer and more just society.

Olatunji Olusanya currently resides in the United Kingdom, where he is actively involved in social commentary, community advocacy, and mentorship. He deploys his wisdom and life lessons to empower future generations.

www.ingramcontent.com/pod-product-compliance
Lightning Source LLC
LaVergne TN
LVHW010219070526
838199LV00062B/4658